FIRST AMERICANS

1995 Engagement Calendar

with 56 Masterworks
of
North American Indian Art

Phil Bellfy
and
Judith Dupré

Random House, Inc.
New York

HILILI KACHINA (Hopi), c. 1920; cottonwood, mineral paints, 17"H (43.2cm.).
No word exists for art or religion in Native American languages; both were inseparable
from life. The Hopi, for example, believe in kachinas, protective spirit-beings who live in the
mountains of northern Arizona, and carve cottonwood dolls such as this one to represent
these benevolent sprits. Once given to Hopi girls to ensure their fertility, kachinas have
been sold to non-Hopi for over a century, despite the objections of tribal members
who believe they are sacred.

Collection: The Museum of Northern Arizona, Flagstaff, AZ.
Photograph: Gene Balzer.

December

DECEMBER 1994

S	M	T	W	T	F	S
				1	2	3
4	5	6	7	8	9	10
11	12	13	14	15	16	17
18	19	20	21	22	23	24
25	26	27	28	29	30	31

Monday
19

1837 Surrender of Ote Emathla (Jumper), influential Seminole chief during the Second Seminole War. He was sent to Oklahoma, where he died of consumption five months later.

Tuesday
20

1936 Birthday of Joe Dan Osceola, Seminole tribal president; first Seminole to graduate from public high school.

Wednesday
21

Winter Solstice (First Day of Winter)

1949 The Laguna Pueblo Constitution, written under the terms of the Indian Reorganization Act, is approved by the Secretary of the Interior.

Thursday
22

1973 The Menominee Restoration Act passed, reversing the effects of termination and restoring federal recognition to the Menominee Tribe of Wisconsin.

Friday
23

1869 Indian Commissioner Parker on the treaty system: "But, because treaties have been made with them… they have become falsely impressed with the notion of national independence."

Saturday
24

1824 Death of notable Choctaw leader Pushmataha, who aided the U.S. forces in the War of 1812. Pushmataha was referred to by Andrew Jackson as the bravest Indian he had ever known.

Sunday
25

Christmas Day

Last quarter of the *Big Winter Moon* of the Seminole.

DECEMBER
JANUARY

DECEMBER 1994

S	M	T	W	T	F	S
				1	2	3
4	5	6	7	8	9	10
11	12	13	14	15	16	17
18	19	20	21	22	23	24
25	26	27	28	29	30	31

JANUARY 1995

S	M	T	W	T	F	S
1	2	3	4	5	6	7
8	9	10	11	12	13	14
15	16	17	18	19	20	21
22	23	24	25	26	27	28
29	30	31				

Monday
26
Boxing Day (Canada)

In December of 1991, the Canadian government announces that it has reached agreement with Inuit leader to create a new province — Nunavut (Our Land) — out of the eastern half of the Northwest Territories.

Tuesday
27

1827 Georgia legislation proclaims: "all the lands . . . of Georgia belong to her absolutely [and] the Indians are tenants at her will." The Indians face removal west three years later.

Wednesday
28

1835 The Seminole chief Osceola and his men ambush and kill a small party of U.S. Army officials, including General Wiley Thompson, who had imprisoned Osceola several months earlier for his refusal to sign a removal treaty.

Thursday
29

1940 Birthday of Robert J. Conley [Cherokee], author of *The Witch of Goingsnake* and other works.

Friday
30

1813 In the waning days of the War of 1812, Iroquois warriors and British soldiers capture town of Buffalo, New York.

Saturday
31

1864 By this date, 8,354 Navajo have completed their forced "Long Walk" to Fort Sumner, New Mexico.

Sunday
1
New Year's Day

New *Frost in the Tepee Moon* of the Lakota.

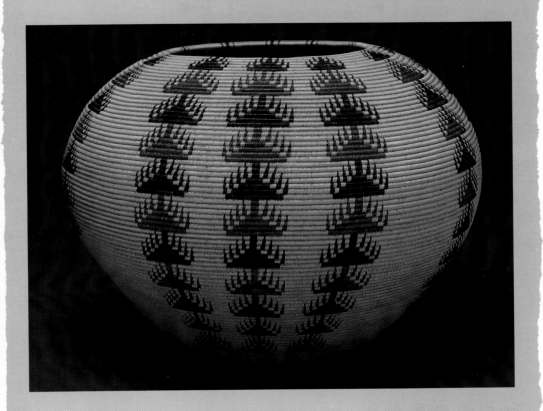

Louisa Keyser/Datsolalee (Washoe), BASKET, DEGIKUP TYPE, c. 1917; willow, bracken root, redbud bark, 12"H, 12 1/4" Diam. (30.5, 31.1 cm.).

In the past, every Native American woman, and to a lesser extent every man, was an artist, skilled in creating designs with grasses, clay, and beads. Most of these artists are unsung, shrouded in anonymity. Basket maker Louisa Keyser, however, once a maid to Abe and Amy Cohn, became internationally famous thanks to the Cohns' shrewd marketing of her work and image. The lionization of Datsolalee, as she was known, caused the price of her works to skyrocket and bestowed upon her a fame that almost overshadowed her superbly fine, remarkably innovative basketry.

Collection: Philbrook Museum of Art, Tulsa, OK.

PLATE (Haida), c. 1888; argillite inset with bone, 13" Diam. (32.5 cm.).

An ancient Haida proverb admonishes the living to walk carefully, for the world is a knife's edge and one could easily fall off. Master carvers, the Haida lived off the coast of British Columbia and created pieces to sell to the New England whalers who plied their waters in the nineteenth century. The skill of the Haida is seen in this platter carved from argillite, a soft carbonaceous shale. The eight heads are carved with a naturalness and humor that suggests caricatures of real subjects; one head nibbles an octopus tentacle, another bites the soft membrane. Though made for outsiders, these works memorialize in stone many old myths.

Collection: Sheldon Jackson Museum, Sitka, AK (I.B.27). Photograph: Stephen E. Hilson.

JANUARY

JANUARY 1995

S	M	T	W	T	F	S
1	2	3	4	5	6	7
8	9	10	11	12	13	14
15	16	17	18	19	20	21
22	23	24	25	26	27	28
29	30	31				

Monday
2

1949 Birthday of Emma Laroque [Métis], Canadian author of *Defeathering the Indian*.

Tuesday
3

Starting in January of 1898, all Tribal Reservation Council decisions require the President's approval.

Wednesday
4

1971 Inauguration of Peter MacDonald as Navajo tribal chairman. He was the first college graduate to lead the Navajo people.

Thursday
5

1975 President Ford signs a bill that cedes 185,000 acres of federal land to the Havasupai of Arizona.

Friday
6

In January of 1863, General Patrick Connor leads his men in an unprovoked attack against the Shoshoni village of Chief Bear Hunter at Bear River, Utah. Over 200 Shoshoni are killed.

Saturday
7

1988 Saying that the organization has been so successful that "it worked itself out of a job," AIM co-founder Russell Means announces his retirement from the group.

Sunday
8

First quarter of the *Hard to Get a Living Moon* of the Malecite.

JANUARY

JANUARY 1995

S	M	T	W	T	F	S
1	2	3	4	5	6	7
8	9	10	11	12	13	14
15	16	17	18	19	20	21
22	23	24	25	26	27	28
29	30	31				

Monday

9

1789 The Treaty of Fort Stanwix. Signed by the leaders of the Iroquois Confederacy at Fort Harmer. This treaty establishes the precedent of paying native people for their ceded land.

Tuesday

10

1992 Death of Jim Pepper [Sioux], the great jazz saxophonist, in Portland, Oregon.

Wednesday

11

1977 U.S. Interior Department issues a report which states that the Passamaquoddy and Penobscot claims to 10.5 million acres in Maine are valid.

Thursday

12

1920 Birthday of Bill Reid [Haida], artist, craftsman, and author of the book of Haida stories *Raven Steals the Light*.

Friday

13

1977 In the face of opposition from the Crow of southern Montana, the Secretary of the Interior revokes a number of leases of Crow lands rich in coal. The revoked leases would have paid the Crow tribe only 17.5 cents a ton in royalties.

Saturday

14

1916 Tohono O'odham (Papago) reservation established in southern Arizona.

Sunday

15

Martin Luther King Jr.'s Birthday

1987 The Inuit and the Dene agree to a partition of the Canadian Northwest Territories into two separate homelands: Nunavut for the Inuit in the east, and Denendeh for the Dene Indians in the west.

Nellie Gates (Standing Rock Sioux), TRAVELING CASE, c. 1903–7; traveling case, glass and metallic beads, metal case fittings, and hide, 16"L, 13"H (40.6, 33 cm.).

The use of seeds, shells, and bones as decorative elements was
supplanted by brilliantly colored European glass beads, which were more easily applied.
Beads were an important item of trade especially for the nomadic Plains Indians who
displayed their wealth primarily through the embellishment of their possessions. Traditional
arts changed by the mid-1800s when many Native Americans were forced to live on
reservations. With hunting sharply curtailed, bead embroidery replaced hide painting as the
dominant decorative technique. Nellie Gates made this handsome traveling case as a wedding
gift to her grandson, J. A. Archambault. It is remarkable for both the complexity of its
imagery and elaborate beadwork.

Collection: Masco Corporation. Photograph courtesy of Sotheby's, New York.

Darren Vigil-Gray (Jicarilla Apache/Kiowa Apache), NOCTURNAL DANCER, 1992; oil on paper, 44 x 33" (111.8 x 83.2 cm.).

Vigil-Gray's paintings mix elements of Native American and European cultures, combining the influences of his childhood upbringing on the Jicarilla Apache Reservation in northern New Mexico with those of a wide range of Indian and European painters, including T. C. Cannon, Fritz Scholder, Francis Bacon, and Henri Matisse. This painting depicts a flamboyantly attired Apache impersonating a Gan, a mountain spirit thought to ward off evil spirits.

Collection: Roskilda Rock Fest, Denmark. Photograph: Jamie Hart.

JANUARY

JANUARY 1995

S	M	T	W	T	F	S
1	2	3	4	5	6	7
8	9	10	11	12	13	14
15	16	17	18	19	20	21
22	23	24	25	26	27	28
29	30	31				

Monday
16
Martin Luther King Jr.'s Birthday Observed

Full *Great Spirit Moon* of the Chippewa.

Tuesday
17

1881 Death of mixed-blood Choctaw chief Peter Pitchlynn, who was chief during the Removal period.

Wednesday
18

1863 After being led to a false peace council, Mangus Coloradas, important Apache war chief who joined with Cochise to raid settlements throughout the Southwest, is killed by soldiers after being tortured.

Thursday
19

1876 General William Tecumseh Sherman states that the civilization of the Indian "has been done by the influence of the Army stationed in their midst, who are, in my opinion, now and have always been the best friends the Indians have had."

Friday
20

1969 St. Regis Mohawks on the U.S.-Canada border vote to send a delegation to the United Nations to demand that the Canadian government recognize the Jay Treaty of 1794, which gives native people the right to pass goods duty-free across the border.

Saturday
21

The Kuskokwim Natives of Alaska file a suit in January of 1969 against Alaskan governor Walter Hickel seeking to reverse his decision to halt the sale of fish by native people to a Japanese company.

Sunday
22

1992 Two Mohawk warriors are convicted of 29 charges (including weapons charges and aggravated assault) stemming from the 1990 Oka incident. Ronald Cross receives a sentence of four years and Gordon Lazore receives 23 months.

JANUARY

JANUARY 1995

S	M	T	W	T	F	S
1	2	3	4	5	6	7
8	9	10	11	12	13	14
15	16	17	18	19	20	21
22	23	24	25	26	27	28
29	30	31				

Monday
23

Last quarter of the *Departing to Hunt Reindeer Moon* of the Point Barrow Eskimo.

Tuesday
24

1826 In the first of a series of removal treaties, the Creek agree to cede their lands in Georgia and move west.

Wednesday
25

1982 Citing an inherent right of sovereignty, the U.S. Supreme Court rules that Indian tribes have the right to impose taxes on the minerals extracted from their lands.

Thursday
26

1926 Birthday of Robert Burnette [Rosebud Sioux], Indian activist, tribal leader, and co-author of the book *The Road to Wounded Knee*, which chronicles the events leading to the takeover of Wounded Knee, South Dakota, in 1973.

Friday
27

1983 After hearing Secretary of the Interior James Watt blame the problems of Indian reservations on "the failures of socialism," the National Congress of American Indians calls for his resignation.

Saturday
28

1992 Death of Lorraine Doebbler [Lower Elwha Klallam], a highly successful Indian educator who reduced a 98% student dropout rate at her school in 1967 to nearly zero by the time of her death.

Sunday
29

1881 Surrender of Iron Dog and his followers at Camp Poplar River, Montana.

Factory No. 7. 5th Dist. N. J.

Kiowa Woman and Papoose

ZIRA CIGARETTES

CIGARETTE PREMIUM, early twentieth century; silk, 3 1/4 x 2 1/2" (8.3 x 6.4 cm.).

———————

In the 1880s, color reproductions on card stock of portraits of well-known Indian chieftains such as Sitting Bull, Red Cloud, Black Hawk, and Geronimo were used as tobacco premiums to promote cigarettes. Later ones, such as this Kiowa Woman and Papoose premium issued by the makers of Zira cigarettes, were printed on silk to appeal to female smokers who used them in crafts or as tabletop decorations.

Private collection.

NAVAJO SERAPE, 1860s; handspun wool, 67 x 44" (170.2 x 111.8 cm.).

Change and synthesis describe the Navajo approach to their world and weaving.
The women were the weavers and incorporated a wide range of influences into their
work–here the diamonds of the Mexican Saltillo weaving are combined with a Plains
Indian hand motif. What was important to the weaver was the process of weaving itself,
which is considered sacred and a paradigm of womanhood. In her transformation of
humble materials into objects of beauty, a weaver could imitate the mythic, regenerative
Changing Woman or Mother Earth.

JANUARY
FEBRUARY

JANUARY 1995

S	M	T	W	T	F	S
1	2	3	4	5	6	7
8	9	10	11	12	13	14
15	16	17	18	19	20	21
22	23	24	25	26	27	28
29	30	31				

FEBRUARY 1995

S	M	T	W	T	F	S
			1	2	3	4
5	6	7	8	9	10	11
12	13	14	15	16	17	18
19	20	21	22	23	24	25
26	27	28				

Monday
30

New *Changeable Moon* of the Blackfoot.

Tuesday
31

1786 The Shawnee, valiant enemy of the American forces in the War of Independence, cede land to, and sign peace treaty with, the new U.S. government.

Wednesday
1

Kennebec Chief Egeremet is killed in February of 1696 while approaching Fort Pemaquid, Maine, under a flag of truce.

Thursday
2

1987 Danny Joe, former chief of the Selkirk Indian Band, wins a seat in the Yukon territorial election, giving his party, the New Democrats, its first majority in the territorial legislature.

Friday
3

1992 Death of William Hallett, who directed the BIA from 1979 to 1981, in a car accident near Bemidji, Minnesota.

Saturday
4

1990 The Colombian government recognizes native rights to 69,000 square miles of the Colombian Amazon basin. The area is home to 55,000 native people.

Sunday
5

1948 Birthday of Jeannette Armstrong [Okanogan], Canadian poet and author of the novel *Slash*.

FEBRUARY

FEBRUARY 1995

S	M	T	W	T	F	S
			1	2	3	4
5	6	7	8	9	10	11
12	13	14	15	16	17	18
19	20	21	22	23	24	25
26	27	28				

Monday

6

1976 The Royal Canadian Mounted Police arrest Leonard Peltier, wanted in connection with the murder of two FBI agents on the Oglala Sioux reservation.

Tuesday

7

First quarter of the *Moon When the Olachen Run* of the Kwakiutl.

Wednesday

8

1990 For the first time in Ontario history, five Manitoulin Island bands and the Ontario government reach a settlement of longstanding land claims. The bands receive over $5 million in land and cash to purchase other land lost since 1862.

Thursday

9

1961 John O. Crow [Cherokee] named as acting director of the BIA, becoming the first person of Indian descent to be director since Eli Parker, who was appointed director in 1871.

Friday

10

1763 Treaty of Versailles concluded, ending the French and Indian War, which destroyed France as an American power.

Saturday

11

In February of 1929, a law is passed which authorizes state employees to enter Indian reservations to enforce compulsory school attendance of Indian children.

Sunday

12

Lincoln's Birthday

1974 Trial begins for Russell Means and Dennis Banks on federal charges stemming from the takeover of Wounded Knee in 1973.

**THREE SILVER BROOCHES (Seneca Iroquois), L to R: Masonic type,
1937; 1 1/2 x 1 13/16" (4 x 4.6 cm.); Octagonal type, collected in 1928;
15/16 x 15/16" (2.3 cm.); Masonic type, c. 1880; 1 1/2 x 1 15/16" (3.8 x 4.8 cm.).**

———————

European silversmiths originally made silver ornaments to trade for furs or to give
to chieftains as tokens of political alliance. As a result, Iroquois men and women began
wearing silver brooches as clothing fasteners and as decorations, sometimes as many
as two to three hundred at a time. By the mid-1800s, every Iroquois village boasted
a skilled and imaginative silversmith.

Collection: Rochester Museum & Science Center, Rochester, NY. Photograph: Brian D. Fox.

BLACK ON WHITE BOWL (Mimbres, New Mexico),
c. 900–1100; 10 1/2" Diam. (26.7 cm.).

Part of an ancient, thriving cultural and trading network in southwestern New Mexico,
the Mimbres people created uniquely figurative pottery. The pottery is extraordinary
for the magnificence and delicacy of its painted designs that, one thousand years later,
still have the power to amaze. This image of a young couple wrapped in a blanket is an
example of the lively humanity and peculiar humor of many Mimbres pieces.

Collection: National Museum of the American Indian, Smithsonian Institution.

FEBRUARY

FEBRUARY 1995

S	M	T	W	T	F	S
			1	2	3	4
5	6	7	8	9	10	11
12	13	14	15	16	17	18
19	20	21	22	23	24	25
26	27	28				

Monday
13

1929 Birthday of Robert Chute [Sokoki Band Abenaki], poet and author of *Thirteen Moons* and *When Grandmother Decides to Die*.

Tuesday
14
Valentine's Day

1973 Canadian government agrees to negotiate with the Indians of the Yukon Territory over land and mineral rights. These native people never signed treaties with the Canadian government.

Wednesday
15

Full *Light of Day Returning Moon* of the Osage.

Thursday
16

1875 U.S. Army campaign against the Kiowa, Cheyenne, and Comanche in Indian Territory ends.

Friday
17

1793 Death of Alexander McGillivray, Creek Wind Clan chief, British general, Spanish colonel, and American brigadier general, who, despite his many roles, always worked in the best interest of his tribe.

Saturday
18

1861 Arapaho and Cheyenne cede most of eastern Colorado, which was guaranteed to them in an 1851 treaty, but they retain the right to hunt on the ceded land.

Sunday
19

1974 U.S. Supreme Court upholds election of a Navajo as county supervisor. Opponents had claimed that because he lived on the reservation and was immune to "normal legal process," he was ineligible to serve in county government.

FEBRUARY

FEBRUARY 1995

S	M	T	W	T	F	S
			1	2	3	4
5	6	7	8	9	10	11
12	13	14	15	16	17	18
19	20	21	22	23	24	25
26	27	28				

Monday
20
President's Day

1993 Death of Sam Cagey, Lummi Indian leader who founded a health center and established the tribe's two fish hatcheries.

Tuesday
21

1835 Formal acceptance by the U.S. Senate of treaty by which the Potawatomi, Ottawa, and Chippewa cede land, including that of Chicago, to the U.S. government.

Wednesday
22
Washington's Birthday

Last quarter of the *Moon of the Snow Storm* of the Tsekehne.

Thursday
23

1875 Surrender of the Kiowa chiefs Lone Wolf, Red Otter, and Lean Bull to the officers of the Tenth Cavalry.

Friday
24

"The instruction of the Indians in [their own tongue] is not only of no use to them, it is detrimental to the cause of their education and civilization. . . ." —Indian Commissioner John Atkins, in 1887, on the use of native language in the schools.

Saturday
25

1642 Dutch settlers of Staten Island brutally massacre 120 Wecquaesgeek Indian men, women, and children asleep in their wigwams.

Sunday
26

1855 Sixteen chiefs petition Washington to remain on ancestral lands in Upper Michigan: "We love the spot where our forefathers' bones are laid, and we desire that our bones may rest beside theirs also."

SERPENT MOUND (Adena), 500 B.C.–A.D. 700.

Ohio's great Serpent Mound was made by the ancient Adena about 2,000 years ago and is a quarter mile long, twenty feet wide, and five feet high. The first archeological survey of this site, and about 200 others scattered throughout the Southeast, was made in the 1840s by Ohioans Ephraim G. Squier and Edwin H. Davis. No one knows why these effigy mounds were built, though they were well known in the nineteenth century when many romantic souls believed them to be not the work of Native Americans but of a "lost race" of émigrés from Greece, Persia, Norway, or, perhaps, the mythical island of Atlantis. The Adenas' sophisticated society flourished, aided by master farmers who raised corn, squash, beans, and tobacco.

Collection: Ohio Historical Society.

**POWDER HORN (Penobscot), late eighteenth century; horn,
handmade nails, wood plug, 12"L (30.5 cm.).**

This engraved powder horn is the elegant legacy of the Penobscot of Maine who once
flourished in the woodlands of the Northeast. Although native people on the Atlantic
Coast were friendly to incoming Europeans and taught them the skills of survival,
conflicts arose as the French, Dutch, and English vied for their land. Recently, federal
courts have given settlements to the Penobscot and other tribes whose land was
taken illegally in the early days of the United States.

Collection: Trotta-Bono American Indian Art.

FEBRUARY
MARCH

FEBRUARY 1995

S	M	T	W	T	F	S
			1	2	3	4
5	6	7	8	9	10	11
12	13	14	15	16	17	18
19	20	21	22	23	24	25
26	27	28				

MARCH 1995

S	M	T	W	T	F	S
			1	2	3	4
5	6	7	8	9	10	11
12	13	14	15	16	17	18
19	20	21	22	23	24	25
26	27	28	29	30	31	

Monday
27

1949 The American Red Cross appropriates $250,000 to aid blizzard-stricken native people in Arizona, New Mexico, and Utah.

Tuesday
28

1953 Birthday of Karoniaktatie (Alex Jacobs), Mohawk author of *Migration Tears*, a book of poems.

Wednesday
1

Ash Wednesday

New *Egg Laying Moon* of the Penobscot.

Thursday
2

1972 Stanford University of Palo Alto, California, drops an American Indian symbol, used since 1930 for its athletic teams, after protest from native students.

Friday
3

1945 Birthday of Emerson Blackhorse Mitchell [Navajo], author of *Miracle Hill* and *Grandmother's Mistake.*

Saturday
4

1985 The U.S. Supreme Court rules that the Oneida Nation is entitled to sue over land lost through an illegal sale for 50 cents an acre in 1975. The Oneida claim involves about 100,000 acres.

Sunday
5

1496 The English king Henry VII grants to Henry Cabot the right to "subdue, occupy, and possess" any lands that he may find in the New World.

MARCH

MARCH 1995

S	M	T	W	T	F	S
			1	2	3	4
5	6	7	8	9	10	11
12	13	14	15	16	17	18
19	20	21	22	23	24	25
26	27	28	29	30	31	

Monday
6

1968 The National Council on Indian Opportunity is created by executive order.

Tuesday
7

1945 Birthday of Roxy Gordon [Choctaw], author of the book *Breeds*.

Wednesday
8

1971 The Union of Nova Scotia Indians, claiming immunity under Canada's federal Indian Act, announces that it will no longer pay provincial taxes on reservation lands.

Thursday
9

First quarter of the *Black Specks on the Snow Moon* of the Fraser Lake Carrier.

Friday
10

In March of 1990, the U.S. Department of Education charters the Indian Nations at Risk Task Force and charges it to study the state of native education and to devise recommendations for its improvement.

Saturday
11

1975 For the first time in Canadian history, natives take control of a legislative assembly when voters send nine native people (out of 15) to the Northwest Territories Assembly.

Sunday
12

1848 Death of Tahchee, a Western Cherokee chief who was a member of the first group of Cherokee that moved west from their traditional homeland. He resisted government attempts to move his followers even farther west in 1824.

**Stephen Mopope (Kiowa), KIOWA CHIEF, 1931; watercolor,
11 1/2 x 8" (29.2 x 20.3 cm.).**

Stephen Mopope was one of five Kiowa artists who were encouraged to paint by Susie Peters, a field matron at St. Michael's Mission School in Anadarko. The dynamic decorative painting of the five formed the basis of the Oklahoma School of painting and has since inspired generations of American Indian painters. In 1939, Mopope's work was used to publicize the Golden Gate International Exposition in San Francisco, the first important international exposition of American Indian art.

**G. Peter Jemison (Seneca), THE CARDINAL VISITS SAN FRANCISCO, 1989;
oil on canvas, 40 x 50" (101.6 x 127 cm.).**

The feathered ceremonial Seneca cap in this painting informs the apparent cheerful
diplomacy of the two birds. At one time, the five Iroquois nations—Mohawk, Oneida,
Onondaga, Cayuga, and Seneca—were enemies who formed a powerful political alliance
called the League of Iroquois in order to better protect themselves from invaders. The
larger problems of the tribes were decided by the League Council, which was composed
of the chiefs from each nation appointed by the women. Benjamin Franklin and Thomas
Jefferson befriended the Iroquois and incorporated much of what they learned from
them into the democracy described by the United States Constitution. The League later
became the Six Nations when the Tuscaroras joined them.

Collection of the artist.

MARCH

MARCH 1995

S	M	T	W	T	F	S
			1	2	3	4
5	6	7	8	9	10	11
12	13	14	15	16	17	18
19	20	21	22	23	24	25
26	27	28	29	30	31	

Monday

13

1952 Birthday of Anita Endrezze [Yaqui], poet and author of the book *At the Helm of Twilight*.

Tuesday

14

1493 Christopher Columbus writes: "I did not find, as some of us had expected, any cannibals amongst them, but on the contrary, men of great deference and kindness."

Wednesday

15

1913 Death of prominent Brule Sioux chief, warrior, and orator Hollow-Horn Bear. His portrait was used on the 14-cent postage stamp issued in 1922.

Thursday

16

Purim

Full *Raccoon Breeding Moon* of the Winnebago.

Friday

17

St. Patrick's Day

1775 Richard Henderson, a North Carolina judge, buys a vast tract of Cherokee land for the Transylvania Land Company. The purchase is later declared invalid, but the land cession is not reversed.

Saturday

18

Seneca chief Red Jacket, in a March 1792 speech to the U.S. Senate: "Our seats were once large, and yours were very small. [But now] we have scarcely a place left to spread our blankets. You have got our country, but you are not satisfied."

Sunday

19

1973 As a show of support for the occupiers at Wounded Knee and to protest media portrayal of native people, Marlon Brando in March of 1973 declines his Oscar for his role in the movie *The Godfather*.

MARCH

MARCH 1995

S	M	T	W	T	F	S
			1	2	3	4
5	6	7	8	9	10	11
12	13	14	15	16	17	18
19	20	21	22	23	24	25
26	27	28	29	30	31	

Monday

20

Vernal Equinox (First Day of Spring)

1961 President John F. Kennedy requests that Congress appropriate $20 million to build schools for 5,000 Native American and Inuit children.

Tuesday

21

In the case of *U.S. v. Wheeler*, decided in March of 1978, the Supreme Court affirms "that the Indian tribes have not given up their full sovereignty. . . . Until Congress acts, the tribes retain their existing sovereign powers."

Wednesday

22

1970 Four native people are arrested after a four-day sit-in at a BIA office near Denver. The sit-in is aimed at BIA employment practices and demands that more native people be employed by the BIA.

Thursday

23

Last quarter of the *Greasewood Fence Moon* of the Hopi.

Friday

24

1990 Brazilian President Fernando Collor orders the destruction of illegal airstrips built by gold miners in the Amazon jungle. The action is designed to protect the Yanomami.

Saturday

25

1886 *The Progress*, the first newspaper published on the White Earth Reservation, begins publication. The press is immediately confiscated and publication suspended for six months.

Sunday

26

1885 Date marking first clash between the Royal Canadian Mounted Police and the South Saskatchewan Métis in the ill-fated Reil Rebellion.

JACKET (Cree or Cree-Métis), 1890–1910; smoked moose hide, cotton, silk thread, bead braid, 36 5/8"L (93 cm.).

The Cree-Métis were mixed-blood descendants of European fur traders and upper-Plains tribes, and their clothing reflected the interaction of the two cultures. Métis jackets, cut from hide and tailored with cuffs and buttonholes, were embroidered with exuberant Victorian florals in what is known as the "Norway House Style." Larger-than-life characters such as George Armstrong Custer and "Buffalo Bill" Cody favored these distinctive furnishings.

Collection: Haffenreffer Museum of Anthropology, Brown University. Photograph: Richard Hurley.

**LIDDED BASKET (Aleut), before 1896; barley and pea grasses,
9"H, 7 1/2"D (22.8, 19 cm.).**

Long apprenticeships, involving hours of watching and assisting, were required of women
learning to make highly prized Arctic baskets. Basket making required knowing what
grasses could be used and at what times of the year they could be harvested. It involved
ceremony as well, with prayers and songs offered before and during the weaving. Lastly,
it involved technical knowledge of twining. Arctic women also wove hats, socks, and
mittens from grass.

Collection: Department of Anthropology, Smithsonian Institution (78.6101).

MARCH
APRIL

MARCH 1995

S	M	T	W	T	F	S
			1	2	3	4
5	6	7	8	9	10	11
12	13	14	15	16	17	18
19	20	21	22	23	24	25
26	27	28	29	30	31	

APRIL 1995

S	M	T	W	T	F	S
						1
2	3	4	5	6	7	8
9	10	11	12	13	14	15
16	17	18	19	20	21	22
23	24	25	26	27	28	29
30						

Monday
27

1973 The U.S. Supreme Court rules that Arizona cannot impose a state income tax on income earned by native people on their reservation.

Tuesday
28

1993 Death of popular country and western singer Buddy Red Bow [Lakota]. Red Bow was also a movie actor who appeared in the movies *Young Guns* and *Powwow Highway*, and was a consultant for the movie *Thunderheart*.

Wednesday
29

1990 The Canadian Human Rights Commission issues a report strongly critical of the federal government's treatment of Canada's native population.

Thursday
30

New *Harvest Kehkheet Root Moon* of the Nez Percé.

Friday
31

1959 Representatives from 10 U.S. Indian tribes form the United Indian Nation in an attempt to halt white encroachment onto their lands.

Saturday
1

1950 Birthday of Beverly Hungry Wolf [Blood], author of *The Ways of My Grandmother*.

Sunday
2

1513 Juan Ponce de León sights Florida and lands near site of present-day St. Augustine.

APRIL

APRIL 1995

S	M	T	W	T	F	S
						1
2	3	4	5	6	7	8
9	10	11	12	13	14	15
16	17	18	19	20	21	22
23	24	25	26	27	28	29
30						

Monday
3

1980 Government of Maine and the Penobscot and Passamaquoddy Indians settle land claims in the state of Maine. The tribes are to receive $81.5 million.

Tuesday
4

1977 United States Supreme Court rules that laws passed by Congress which require the Sioux to cede their lands on the Rosebud reservation in South Dakota are valid, despite contrary provisions of their 1868 treaty.

Wednesday
5

1973 Thirty-seven day confrontation at Wounded Knee ends with the signing of an agreement in which the government agrees to examine Sioux treaty rights. Due to government inaction, the agreement never takes effect.

Thursday
6

1973 Director Constantin Costa-Gavras on the Indian in film: "The old Hollywood films are political. They rationalized the extermination of the American Indians. . . . If you saw Indians in the film, you knew that, at the end, they would die."

Friday
7

First quarter of the *Moon When the Snow Disappears from the High Ground* of the Shuswap.

Saturday
8

1937 Birthday of Bernelda Wheeler [Cree-Ojibway Métis], author of the books of traditional tales *A Friend Called Chum* and *I Can't Have Bannock, But the Beaver Has a Dam.*

Sunday
9

Palm Sunday

1981 Members of the Bigstone Cree end a 250-mile march to Edmonton, Alberta. The march is designed to highlight the economic plight of the Bigstone Cree suffering a 60% unemployment rate in northern Alberta.

**EARTHEN VASE (Acoma), early nineteenth century; earthenware, paint,
12"H (30.4 cm.).**

———

The ancestral home of the Acoma, colloquially known as "Sky City," sits high atop a
mesa in western New Mexico. This pueblo has been inhabited since A.D. 1200. Pottery
was, and remains, a pervasive influence in the lives of the Pueblo people. At birth newborn
Acoma Indians are bathed in pottery bowls, and when they die they are buried with pots.
Known for being especially fine and thin-walled due to the properties of the local clay,
Acoma pottery is both geometric and representational in design. The location
of the clay remains undisclosed; even today, no outsiders are taken there.
This is the only known six-color historic jar.

Collection: Department of Anthropology, Smithsonian Institution (86.11555).

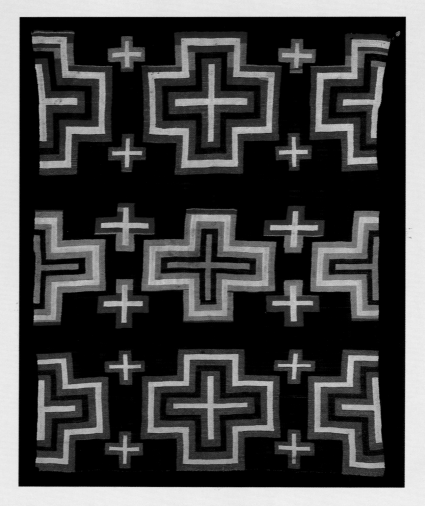

MOKI SERAPE (Navajo), 1865–75; handspun wool, 73 x 56" (185.4 x 142.2 cm.).

The Navajo of the Southwest have always been known for their ability to absorb and redefine the cultures surrounding them. They developed blankets in the Serape Style by drawing on Spanish, rather than Pueblo, precedents, unconsciously adapting and integrating diverse elements. Here we see the influence of the cruciform shape as distributed, if not introduced, by the proselytizing Spanish in the form of rosaries and metal crosses. The Moki Serape with crosses was revived at the turn of the century by the trader Lorenzo Hubbell.

Collection: Anthony Berlant, Santa Monica.

APRIL

APRIL 1995

S	M	T	W	T	F	S
						1
2	3	4	5	6	7	8
9	10	11	12	13	14	15
16	17	18	19	20	21	22
23	24	25	26	27	28	29
30						

Monday

10

1923 Birthday of Popovi Da, artist, craftsman, businessman, and Pueblo leader.

Tuesday

11

1775 The town of Boonesborough, Kentucky, founded on land sold to the Transylvania Company by the Cherokee. The town is subsequently attacked several times by the Shawnee.

Wednesday

12

1968 The Tigua Pueblo people of the northwest corner of Texas are recognized by the federal government.

Thursday

13

1980 The Citizen's Party, meeting in convention in Cleveland, Ohio, chooses LaDonna Harris [Comanche], founder and president of Americans for Indian Opportunity, to be their vice presidential candidate.

Friday

14

Good Friday

1756 Pennsylvania governor Morris's declaration of war on the Delaware Indians states: "For the scalp of every male *Indian* enemy . . . the *Sum of One Hundred and Thirty Pieces of Eight*."

Saturday

15

Full *Big Wind Moon* of the Zuni Pueblo.

Sunday

16

Easter

1648 Jesuit priest Jerome Lalemant, on Great Lakes native people: "They are a free people . . . and they submit to their chiefs only so far as it pleases them."

APRIL

APRIL 1995

S	M	T	W	T	F	S
						1
2	3	4	5	6	7	8
9	10	11	12	13	14	15
16	17	18	19	20	21	22
23	24	25	26	27	28	29
30						

Monday

17

Easter Monday (Canada)

1680 Death of Kateri Tekakwitha, the first Indian Roman Catholic nun, from self-inflicted penitential wounds. She has been beatified by the Catholic Church.

Tuesday

18

1879 The civil rights case of *Standing Bear v. Crook* begins. The judge finds that the Ponca chief Standing Bear is indeed a "person" under the law and therefore protected by the Constitution.

Wednesday

19

1891 In the third great opening of land in Indian Territory, 4.3 million acres of Cheyenne and Arapaho land are released to 25,000 white settlers.

Thursday

20

1953 U.S. House of Representatives passes a bill that repeals a ban on selling guns or ammunition to native people.

Friday

21

First Day of Passover

Last quarter of the *Herring Spawning Moon* of the Nootka.

Saturday

22

1978 The Fort Hall, Idaho, reservation council votes to bar non-natives from reservation lands after the U.S. Supreme Court rules that non-natives cannot be tried in tribal courts for crimes committed on reservation property.

Sunday

23

1746 A war party of about 80 Indians attacks a settlement on the Ashuelot River, near present-day Keene, New Hampshire.

**Pa-to-kas-wit (Warm Springs/Cayuse), BAG, 1890–95; hemp,
natural and aniline dyes, 21 x 17" (53.3 x 43.2 cm.).**

———————

Masterpieces of abstract design, soft twined "cornhusk" bags such as this one were woven
by the women of the Columbia Plateau region of the Northwest and used for storing
dried roots. Tribes lived peacefully in an area abundant with food and strategically
located for intertribal commerce on the Columbia River. Plateau designs show the
influences of both Plains and Northwest Coast Indians.

Collection: The Museum at Warm Springs, Oregon.

THOMAS JEFFERSON INDIAN PEACE MEDAL, 1801; silver, 4" Diam. (10.2 cm.).

European countries attempting to curry favor with Indian chieftains presented them with silver medals, a practice continued by the fledgling United States beginning with George Washington's administration. The so-called "peace medals" were highly prized by American Indian chiefs who, if they were not buried with them, bequeathed them to future generations. The medals were issued by every president except John Adams until 1893, when, long after the Indians had been subdued on reservations, the last of the peace medals were struck. On their expeditions west, Lewis and Clark were authorized to bestow this medal on Jefferson's behalf.

Collection: American Numismatic Society, New York.

APRIL

APRIL 1995

S	M	T	W	T	F	S
						1
2	3	4	5	6	7	8
9	10	11	12	13	14	15
16	17	18	19	20	21	22
23	24	25	26	27	28	29
30						

Monday

24

1943 Birthday of novelist Thomas King [Cherokee], author of *Medicine River* and other works.

Tuesday

25

1890 Death of Chief Crowfoot of the Canadian Blackfeet: "What is life? It is the flash of a firefly in the night. It is the breath of a buffalo in the winter time. It is as the little shadow that runs across the grass and loses itself in the sunset."

Wednesday

26

In April of 1983, President Ronald Reagan vetoes a bill that would have settled the claims of the Mashantucket Pequot Indian tribe in eastern Connecticut, arguing that the claim for land lost through an illegal sale is a state issue.

Thursday

27

1918 The Coopah reservation in southwest Arizona is established for the Yuma (Quechan) people.

Friday

28

"It is through self-government that a people can maintain the sense of pride and self-worth which is necessary for productive, happy lives. . . . There is no need to sever one's roots." —Brian Mulroney, Canadian Prime Minister, in April of 1985.

Saturday

29

New *Moon of Delicate Leaves* of the Navajo.

Sunday

30

1966 The Senate confirms the appointment of Robert La Follette Bennett [Oneida] as Indian Affairs Commissioner.

MAY

MAY 1995

S	M	T	W	T	F	S
	1	2	3	4	5	6
7	8	9	10	11	12	13
14	15	16	17	18	19	20
21	22	23	24	25	26	27
28	29	30	31			

Monday
1

1974 Ralph Steinhauer [Cree], former chief of the Saddle Lake Band, named Lieutenant Governor of Alberta.

Tuesday
2

1670 The British Crown issues a Royal Charter granting the Hudson's Bay Company ownership of "Rupert's Land," which comprises much of central and northern Canada.

Wednesday
3

1883 Birthday of Charles Bender [Chippewa], major league pitcher who led the American League in strikeouts in 1910, 1911, and 1914. Charlie Bender is the only Native American in the Baseball Hall of Fame.

Thursday
4

1992 Voters in Canada's Northwest Territories approve a plan to create a 772,000-square-mile self-governing homeland for the area's 17,500 Inuit. The new homeland would be called Nunavut, which means "Our Land."

Friday
5

1875 Death of Kicking Bird, Kiowa leader and warrior. Poison is suspected as the cause of his death.

Saturday
6

1986 Donald E. Pelotte, an Abenaki from Maine, ordained as a bishop in the Roman Catholic Church, becoming the first Native American Roman Catholic bishop.

Sunday
7

First quarter of the *Plant Secretly Moon* of the Hano.

FEATHER BONNET (Assiniboine or Gros Ventre), c. 1885; eagle feathers, red cloth, beads, ermine, porcupine hair, and weasel skins, 28"L (71.1 cm.).

Plains Indian culture—buffalo, tipis, and feathers—has become synonymous with all North American Indian art, which is in fact extremely diverse in its use of materials and its designs. Feather headdresses are among the most striking items of Plains regalia. Eagle feathers, symbols of protection and blessings, were once given to warriors who earned the right to wear them by performing courageously; today they are given to those who have accomplished a noble goal. This is a splendid example of a classic "swept-back" headdress.

Collection: Buffalo Bill Historical Center, Cody, WY. Chandler-Pohrt Collection.

MOTHER AND CHILD (Hopi), c. 1880; polychrome cottonwood, 8"H (20.3 cm.).

Wrapped around the shoulders of this Hopi mother is a traditional shawl, or manta, which she clutches tightly to ensure the safety of her tiny baby. No longer a maiden, she wears her hair knotted on her forehead and is dressed in the plump white hide leggings of the Hopi. This unusual sculpture appears to be a tender portrait of a mother and child carved by a proud father. It is not likely a Madonna figure, as the Hopi were especially resistant to the Spanish efforts to convert them to Christianity.

Collection: Christopher Selser, Santa Fe. Photograph: Herb Lotz.

MAY

MAY 1995

S	M	T	W	T	F	S
	1	2	3	4	5	6
7	8	9	10	11	12	13
14	15	16	17	18	19	20
21	22	23	24	25	26	27
28	29	30	31			

Monday
8

1968 Death in Taos, New Mexico, of John Collier, Commissioner of Indian Affairs during the New Deal administration of Franklin Delano Roosevelt from 1933 to 1945.

Tuesday
9

1951 Birthday of celebrated Creek poet Joy Harjo, author of the poetry collections *She Has Some Horses*, *Secrets from the Center of the World*, and *In Mad Love and War*.

Wednesday
10

1838 U.S. Army General Winfield Scott issues a proclamation demanding that all Cherokee must be on their way west within one month: "To join that part of your people who are already established in prosperity on the other side of the Mississippi."

Thursday
11

A May 1971 agreement between British Columbia and the Canadian government authorizes the Cape Mudge Indians of British Columbia to form Canada's first Indian municipality.

Friday
12

1776 The Continental Congress solicits the aid of Indians to fight the British, offering the Indians soldier's pay, plus bounties. Native warriors largely ignore the plea.

Saturday
13

1992 Ecuador's government grants 148 native communities legal title to more than three million acres in the Amazon River basin.

Sunday
14
Mother's Day

Full *Young Seals Take to the Sea Moon* of the Netchilli.

MAY

MAY 1995

S	M	T	W	T	F	S
	1	2	3	4	5	6
7	8	9	10	11	12	13
14	15	16	17	18	19	20
21	22	23	24	25	26	27
28	29	30	31			

Monday
15

1970 The U.S. Army takes 78 native people into custody after they attempt to enter Fort Lawton, located in a Seattle neighborhood. The native people wish to create a cultural center on the abandoned site.

Tuesday
16

1947 Chief Swimming Eel (Franklin Bearce) of Stamford, Connecticut, calls for the United Nations to investigate charges that the Canadian government is violating provisions of the Jay Treaty of 1794.

Wednesday
17

Ojibway people and Wisconsin state officials reached an agreement in May of 1991 on their 17-year-old dispute over fishing and gathering rights on off-reservation treaty lands.

Thursday
18

1642 Sieur de Maisonneuve founds the city of Montreal.

Friday
19

1882 Birthday of Clinton Rickard, Tuscarora tribal leader.

Saturday
20

1506 Christopher Columbus dies in Valladolid, Spain, neglected and almost forgotten, never fully realizing the importance of his discoveries.

Sunday
21

Last quarter of the *Moon When the Snow Crusts at Night* of the Chandalar Kutchin.

BEE MASK (Kwakiutl), c. 1904; wood, feathers, cloth, brass, twigs, animal hair, 16 15/16"L, 6 11/16"D (43, 17 cm.).

Indians of the Northwest Coast still hold special gatherings called potlatches to celebrate the times when an individual is given a new name. In the past the wealthiest families hosted potlatches that lasted several weeks. Guests watched dances, heard family histories, feasted on salmon and berry cakes, and were given lavish gifts. This bee mask, with spiky stingers emanating from it, was worn by a potlatch dancer who would run about imitating the bee's erratic flight patterns, pausing only to "sting" members of the audience.

Collection: American Museum of Natural History, Courtesy Department of Library Services (4560/2). Photograph: Lynton Gardiner.

Arthur Amiotte (Oglala Sioux), SIX WOMEN, 1988; acrylic on canvas with collage, 21 x 25" (53.3 x 63.5 cm.).

Long accustomed to communicating ideas in pictures—as evidenced by prehistoric pictographs and paintings on tipis, buffalo robes, and shields—the Plains Indians easily adapted the new art materials that often accompanied white settlers. These included graphite, colored pencils, crayon, and paper; the latter was often in the form of accountants' lined ledger books, which eventually gave name to the genre known as ledger art. In addition to being a direct visual descendant of ledger art, this contemporary work makes commentary on the contrasting ideals, and idealization, of feminine beauty.

Photograph courtesy American Indian Contemporary Art, San Francisco.

MAY

MAY 1995

S	M	T	W	T	F	S
	1	2	3	4	5	6
7	8	9	10	11	12	13
14	15	16	17	18	19	20
21	22	23	24	25	26	27
28	29	30	31			

Monday

22

Victoria Day (Canada)

1798 The Chippewa cede 28,000 acres in Ontario, including Toronto, for £101.

Tuesday

23

1895 Two hundred thousand acres of Kickapoo lands in Indian Territory opened to settlers.

Wednesday

24

1991 The Mashantucket Pequots of Connecticut win federal approval to open a casino near New London. It is the East Coast's first casino outside of Atlantic City.

Thursday

25

1992 Led by AIM activists, 500 people march on Leavenworth prison in Kansas to demand freedom for Leonard Peltier, convicted of the murder of two FBI agents on the Oglala reservation in 1975.

Friday

26

1948 Apaches of New Mexico and Oklahoma file an $8 million claim against the U.S. for imprisonment in the late 1800s and for lands lost to whites in 1877.

Saturday

27

1941 Birthday of poet Simon J. Ortiz [Acoma Pueblo], author of the book of poems *From Sand Creek* and other works.

Sunday

28

1867 Interior Secretary Orville H. Browning: "The War Department seems bent on general war and will probably force all the Indians into it."

MAY

JUNE

MAY 1995

S	M	T	W	T	F	S
	1	2	3	4	5	6
7	8	9	10	11	12	13
14	15	16	17	18	19	20
21	22	23	24	25	26	27
28	29	30	31			

JUNE 1995

S	M	T	W	T	F	S
				1	2	3
4	5	6	7	8	9	10
11	12	13	14	15	16	17
18	19	20	21	22	23	24
25	26	27	28	29	30	

Monday
29
Memorial Day

New *Strawberry Moon* of the Teton Sioux.

Tuesday
30

1968 As part of the Poor People's Campaign in Washington, D.C., 150 native people and their supporters storm the Supreme Court building in an effort to present their case on Indian fishing rights. The justices refuse to meet the Indian delegation.

Wednesday
31

1538 The first of Hernando de Soto's 1,000 *conquistadors* land on the Florida coast, beginning a three-year expedition of pillage in search of gold.

Thursday
1

1868 New Mexico Navajo sign the Treaty of Bosque Redondo with the U.S. government and are permitted to return to a portion of their ancestral lands.

Friday
2

1875 Surrender of Quanah Parker and his Comanche followers, ending the era of the free southern Plains Indians.

Saturday
3

1944 Birthday of John Sackett [Athabascan], youngest person to be elected to Alaska legislature.

Sunday
4

1841 Capture of Seminole chief Coacoochee (Wildcat) during a peace parley. Coacoochee and his followers are shipped west in November.

BIRD'S CLAW (Ohio Hopewell Culture), A.D. 200–400; mica, 11"H (28 cm.).

Objects such as this shimmering mica silhouette were the elegant expression of a mortuary cult who built huge earthworks and mounds in the East. While it is not certain why the mounds were built–they may have functioned as lunar or solar observatories–excavations have revealed them to be treasure troves of artifacts made of opulent materials imported from great distances, including exotic minerals, crystal amulets, freshwater pearls, incised shells, and gold and silver jewelry.

Collection: Ohio Historical Society.

**Marcus Amerman (Choctaw), TRAILING-THE-ENEMY AND HIS WIFE, 1988;
beadwork, mixed media, 15 x 12 1/2" (38.1 x 31.8 cm.).**

This poignant contemporary beadwork portrait speaks of a way of life forever lost.
The two million First Americans are often last when it comes to health care, education,
and economic opportunities. Innovative solutions are needed to fight the crippling
unemployment found on many of the 500 reservations in the United States and Canada.
The arts—a vital and familiar tradition for many minorities—remain a logical, though
often neglected, area of economic development.

JUNE

JUNE 1995

S	M	T	W	T	F	S
				1	2	3
4	5	6	7	8	9	10
11	12	13	14	15	16	17
18	19	20	21	22	23	24
25	26	27	28	29	30	

Monday
5

1846 Potawatomi, Chippewa, and Ottawa cede lands in western Iowa. These lands were previously ceded by Sac and Fox, and other tribes.

Tuesday
6

First quarter of the *Young Animal Moon* of the Aleut.

Wednesday
7

1935 The Yavapai reservation is established in central Arizona.

Thursday
8

1975 AIM leader Russell Means is shot by BIA officer during scuffle at Fort Yates, North Dakota. He is later arrested for obstructing the police officer.

Friday
9

1855 The Yakima, and other tribes, cede central Washington State, and the Walla Walla, Cayuse, and Umatilla Indians cede northeast Oregon.

Saturday
10

1941 Birthday of Ssipsis [Penobscot], author of the book of contemporary Maine Indian stories *Molly Molasses and Me*.

Sunday
11

1922 Robert Flaherty's film *Nanook of the North*, depicting the ingenuity and adaptability of the Arctic Eskimo, is released.

JUNE

JUNE 1995
S	M	T	W	T	F	S
				1	2	3
4	5	6	7	8	9	10
11	12	13	14	15	16	17
18	19	20	21	22	23	24
25	26	27	28	29	30	

Monday

12

Full *Moon When the Salmon Come Up* of the Bulkley Carrier.

Tuesday

13

1977 The First International Inuit Circumpolar Conference opens in Barrow, Alaska. The conference is attended by over 200 indigenous people from Alaska, Canada, and Greenland.

Wednesday

14

Flag Day

1971 After being ousted from Alcatraz Island by federal marshals, John Trudell [Sioux] and about 50 other native people take over an abandoned Army missile base near Richmond, California.

Thursday

15

1899 Birthday of Gladys Tantaquidgeon [Mohegan], author, anthropologist, and museum curator

---

Friday

16

1820 Treaty signed at Sault Ste. Marie, Michigan, whereby the Chippewa cede land but retain "right to fish" in perpetuity.

Saturday

17

1954 The Menominee Indian Tribe is terminated by an act of Congress: "The purpose of this Act is to provide for orderly termination of Federal supervision over the property and members of the Menominee Indian Tribe of Wisconsin."

Sunday

18

Father's Day

1934 Congress passes the Wheeler-Howard Act, known as the Indian Reorganization Act, which reverses the policy of allotment and encouraged tribal organization.

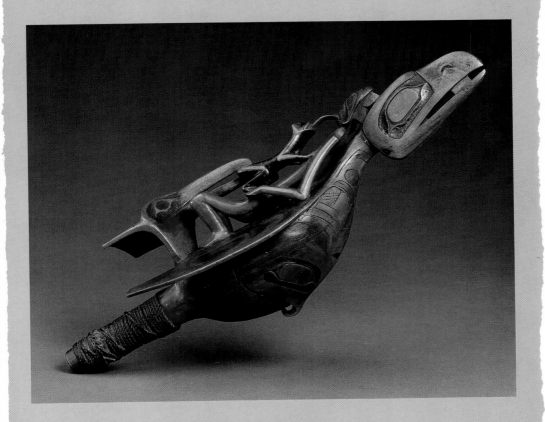

**CEREMONIAL RATTLE (Tlingit), mid- to late nineteenth century;
wood, pigment, cord, 14"L (35.6 cm.).**

At the heart of traditional Native American culture is a fundamental connection to the
natural and spirit worlds. Northwest Coast tribes believed in many spirit-beings which
took the form of animals: this shaman's rattle depicts a raven, frog, and kingfisher. Clan
members owned the rights to display images of the particular animal that helped them
and created the highly stylized wood carving for which the Northwest Coast Indians
are renowned. Ancestry, wealth, and status were very important to these tribes,
as it is to many of us today, and they displayed what they had proudly.

Photograph courtesy of Sotheby's, New York.

BOWL (Luiseño, from La Jolla Reservation), c. 1890; split sumac, natural and black-dyed juncus, grass, 3 3/8" H, 16" Diam. (8.5, 40.5 cm.).

———

Native peoples have bequeathed America an especially rich assortment of intriguing, anthropomorphic symbols of daily life, hunting, and astronomical events. Many of these are found on the implements of everyday life, including baskets. Waterbugs hover between the flower petals on this shallow coiled basket made by a Luiseño woman of southern California. The Luiseño cultivated a great variety of medicinal plants, as well as grasses and roots, to create their baskets.

Collection: Riverside Municipal Museum (A8-100). Photograph: Chris L. Moser from *Native American Basketry of Southern California.*

JUNE

JUNE 1995

S	M	T	W	T	F	S
				1	2	3
4	5	6	7	8	9	10
11	12	13	14	15	16	17
18	19	20	21	22	23	24
25	26	27	28	29	30	

Monday
19

Last quarter of the Montagnais *Flower Moon*.

Tuesday
20

1940 Riley Sunrise [Hopi] refuses to be drafted into the U.S. military: "Justice . . . is dearer to me than life."

Wednesday
21

Summer Solstice (First Day of Summer)

1968 Hundreds of native people and their supporters demonstrate outside the Justice Department to protest restrictions on Indian fishing in Washington State.

Thursday
22

1839 Assassination of John Ridge, his father Major Ridge, and Elias Boudinot (Cherokee author and editor of the *Cherokee Phoenix*) for their roles in the removal of the Cherokee to Oklahoma.

Friday
23

In a statement delivered to the White House in June of 1983, officials of the National Tribal Chairman's Association assail the Reagan administration's failure to fulfill its promise of greater self-government for Indian tribes.

Saturday
24

1899 Birthday of Chief Dan George of the Tselalwatt tribe of British Columbia. Chief Dan George was an eloquent spokesman for native rights and an actor best known for his portrayal of Old Lodge Skins in the 1970 movie *Little Big Man*.

Sunday
25

1969 Canada's Minister of Indian Affairs, John Cretien, announces a government plan to end the legal status of Canada's 237,000 native people. The plan is opposed by all major native groups.

JUNE
JULY

JUNE 1995

S	M	T	W	T	F	S
				1	2	3
4	5	6	7	8	9	10
11	12	13	14	15	16	17
18	19	20	21	22	23	24
25	26	27	28	29	30	

JULY 1995

S	M	T	W	T	F	S
						1
2	3	4	5	6	7	8
9	10	11	12	13	14	15
16	17	18	19	20	21	22
23	24	25	26	27	28	29
30	31					

Monday
26

1975 Two FBI agents, attempting to serve arrest warrants on "a number of individuals," are shot and killed on Oglala Sioux reservation; Little Joe Killsright is also shot dead.

Tuesday
27

New Leaf Opening Moon of the Micmac.

Wednesday
28

1785 At Herkimer, New York, the Oneida and Tuscarora cede their lands in New York State to the U.S. government.

Thursday
29

1930 Birthday of Alice French, Inuit author of *The Restless Nomad.*

Friday
30

1520 Death of Montezuma. Later that night, the Aztecs attack the Spanish and their Tlaxcalan allies and kill about two thirds of them, in what the Spanish call the Noche Triste (Tragic Night).

Saturday
1

Canada Day

1962 Birthday of Canadian dramatist Drew Hayden Taylor [Ojibway], author of the play *Toronto at Dreamer's Rock.*

Sunday
2

1979 U.S. Supreme Court upholds 1854 and 1855 treaties that reserve the right of Indian fishers to 50% of the salmon passing through their treaty waters in Washington State.

CLIFF PALACE, DETAIL (Anasazi), c. 1200–1300;
Mesa Verde National Park, Colorado.

———

Throughout the Southwest are mysterious stone ruins left by the civilizations that
flourished from A.D. 900 to 1300. The masons were Anasazi women who built multiple
dwellings harmoniously placed in relationship to each other and their surroundings.
Having made peace with the harsh sun of their desert home, the Anasazi built thriving
trading networks reaching for hundreds of miles and created vibrantly beautiful art.
Cliff Palace, one of the largest Anasazi cliff dwellings, included 217 rooms and 23 kivas.

Photograph © Chuck Place from *Ancient Walls, Indian Ruins of the Southwest,*
courtesy Fulcrum Publishing, Colorado.

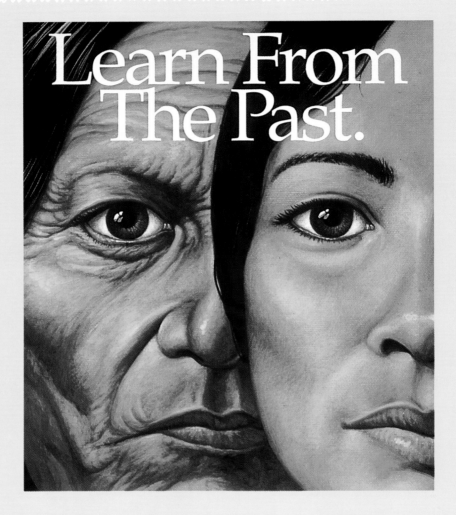

Mark Hess, LEARN FROM THE PAST (detail), 1993; offset lithograph,
68 1/2 x 47 1/2" (174 x 120.7 cm.).

This poster appeared in subways and bus shelters as part of a provocative national
advertising campaign created by Wieden & Kennedy of Portland, Oregon, in an effort
to increase awareness of the twenty-nine American Indian colleges in the United States.
Located on or near reservations, the colleges help preserve native languages, history,
and culture while offering American Indians the opportunity to better themselves
economically without abandoning their homes or traditional way of life.

Courtesy American Indian College Fund, New York.

JULY

JULY 1995

S	M	T	W	T	F	S
						1
2	3	4	5	6	7	8
9	10	11	12	13	14	15
16	17	18	19	20	21	22
23	24	25	26	27	28	29
30	31					

Monday
3

1873 Death of Little Crow [Mdewakanton Sioux], who was a major figure in the 1862 uprising at New Ulm, Minnesota, in which over 400 whites were killed.

Tuesday
4

Independence Day

1776 The Declaration of Independence, recounting the grievances against King George III, says: "He has excited . . . the merciless savages, whose known Rule of Warfare, is an undistinguished Destruction, of all Ages, Sexes, and Conditions."

Wednesday
5

First quarter of the *Moon When Geese Get New Wing Feathers* of the Unalit.

Thursday
6

1967 Death of Chief John Big Tree, the Iroquois whose profile was used in the design of the "Indian Head" nickel, on the Onondaga reservation in New York State.

Friday
7

1979 Two thousand Indian activists and antinuclear demonstrators march through the Black Hills to protest the development of uranium mines in these sacred lands.

Saturday
8

1931 Birthday of composer Louise Ballard [Cherokee-Sioux], who wrote the first modern Indian ballet, *Koshare*, in 1967.

Sunday
9

In July of 1971, the government of Brazil decrees that it is setting up reservations for native people who live near the proposed Trans-Amazon Highway, claiming that the Indians threaten development of the Amazon River basin.

JULY

JULY 1995

S	M	T	W	T	F	S
						1
2	3	4	5	6	7	8
9	10	11	12	13	14	15
16	17	18	19	20	21	22
23	24	25	26	27	28	29
30	31					

Monday
10

1952 The Republican Party platform adopted in convention proclaims that Indians should get "full enjoyment of their rights of citizenship."

Tuesday
11

1869 The U.S. Cavalry, in the Battle of Summit Springs, destroy the Dog Soldiers of the Cheyenne, freeing Kansas for white settlement. Tall Bull, Cheyenne chief, is among those killed.

Wednesday
12

Full *Horse Moon* of the Santa Clara Pueblo.

Thursday
13

1786 The Northwest Ordinance enacted. It states: "The utmost good faith shall always be observed towards the Indians. . . In their property, rights and liberty, they never shall be invaded or disturbed. . . ."

Friday
14

1950 Indian Claims Commission upholds an Indian claim for the first time in its history and awards $3.5 million to the Choctaw and Chickasaw for lands taken illegally at the end of the Civil War.

Saturday
15

1837 A smallpox epidemic reaches the Mandan people in the Dakota Territory. Out of 1,600 Mandans, only 125 survive; many other Plains tribes are affected as well.

Sunday
16

1866 The First Sioux War begins in the Powder River country of Montana.

**CHILKAT SHIRT (Tlingit), n.d.; mountain goat wool and otter fur,
32 7/8 x 25 5/8" (83.5 x 65 cm.).**

———————

The ceremonial robes and shirts made by the Tlingit defy the technical limitations
of weaving, which lends itself to geometric, rather curvilinear, patterns. The whimsical
faces on the shirt are meant to represent the brown bear, a powerful clan symbol,
and her many cubs. This shirt was worn by a male dancer whose kinetic
movements would have emphasized the weaving's explosive design.

Collection: Portland Art Museum, Oregon. Rasmussen Collection of Northwest Coast Indian Art.

SHOULDER BAG (Delaware), c. 1850–60; cloth, seed beads, tin cone pendants, wool yarn, tradecloth, grosgrain ribbon, 31"L (78.7 cm.).

As the nineteenth century progressed, shoulder bags became larger and less utilitarian. Men usually wore multiple bags, criss-crossed over the chest with the pouches resting on the hip, usually at intertribal events, for these festive occasions were a time to assert one's cultural identity. In addition to being a display of wealth, highly decorative bags were a testimony to the love and skill of the devoted wife who made them. The maker's masterful use of negative design space and vibrantly colored beads creates a pulsating, optical effect.

JULY

JULY 1995

S	M	T	W	T	F	S
						1
2	*3*	*4*	*5*	*6*	*7*	*8*
9	*10*	*11*	*12*	*13*	*14*	*15*
16	*17*	*18*	*19*	*20*	*21*	*22*
23	*24*	*25*	*26*	*27*	*28*	*29*
30	*31*					

Monday

17

"The white inhabitants . . . have frequently committed the most unprovoked and direct outrages against the Cherokee Indians . . . dictated by the avaricious desire of obtaining . . . fertile lands." —Secretary of War Henry Knox in July of 1788.

Tuesday

18

1978 AIM leaders, part of the Longest Walk caravan, meet with high government officials to press their demands for fulfillment of treaty rights for native people.

Wednesday

19

Last quarter of the *Corn in Tassel Moon* of the Cherokee.

Thursday

20

1941 Birthday of Inuit writer and poet Fred Bigjim, author of the poetry collection *Sinrock* and other books of poetry and nonfiction.

Friday

21

"Our plea to the world is to help us in our struggle to find a place in the world community where we can exercise our right to self-determination as a distinct people and as a nation." — July 1975 statement of the Dene Nation, Northwest Territories.

Saturday

22

1863 Kit Carson begins his military campaign against the Navajo.

Sunday

23

1838 A delegation of Eastern Cherokee requests that they not be escorted by the Army on their trek west; without Army escort, the removal of 12,000 Cherokee is accomplished peacefully.

JULY

JULY 1995

S	M	T	W	T	F	S
						1
2	3	4	5	6	7	8
9	10	11	12	13	14	15
16	17	18	19	20	21	22
23	24	25	26	27	28	29
30	31					

Monday
24

1952 The Democratic Party platform adopted at convention: "We favor the repeal of all [restrictions] that deny Indians rights or privileges held by citizens generally."

Tuesday
25

1971 Death of John "Chief" Meyers [Cahuilla], major league catcher for New York in the early 1900s, who achieved a .291 lifetime batting average.

Wednesday
26

1829 In the Michigan Territory, the Chippewa, Ottawa, and Potawatomi cede much of their land to the U.S. government.

Thursday
27

New *King Salmon Moon* of the Koyukon.

Friday
28

1864 In the Battle of Killdeer Mountain in northern Dakota Territory, Hunkpapa Sioux defeat whites who were attempting to open Sioux lands to travelers going to Montana, where gold had been discovered.

Saturday
29

1882 The Mexican government agrees to allow U.S. Army troops to pursue Chiricahua Apaches across the border into Mexico.

Sunday
30

1981 United Nations Human Rights Committee finds Canada in breach of International Covenant on Civil and Political Rights due to sex discrimination provisions of the Indian Act.

**Quincy Tahoma (Navajo), IN THE DAYS OF PLENTY, 1946;
watercolor on board, 30 5/8 x 21 5/8" (77.8 x 55 cm.).**

Quincy Tahoma, an energetic practitioner of a highly stylized Indian school of painting
to emerge in the Southwest early in the century, romanticizes the Plains buffalo hunt.
Buffalo was a staple of the Plains Indians, who ingeniously used every part of it for their
survival. When the railroad arrived in the West, on board were hunters who killed
thousands of buffalo, sometimes for the tongue alone, which was considered a delicacy. As
a result, by the end of the 1880s the buffalo was virtually extinct, as was the freedom and
abundance enjoyed by the Plains Indian nations.

Collection: Philbrook Museum of Art, Tulsa, Oklahoma.

Sam Hunter (Hooper Bay), c. 1945; wood, pigment, 26"L x 15"W (66 x 38.1 cm.).

Inspired by dream visions, shamans carved the masks that played an integral role in the
ceremonies of Bering Sea Eskimos. Incoming missionaries, who deemed such masks pagan,
frequently had them destroyed. In 1945, Alfred and Elma Milotte were commissioned by
Walt Disney to make a film on Alaska and hired the carvers of Hooper Bay to recreate from
memory their ancestral masks. After filming, the missionaries began burning the new masks;
the Milottes were able to rescue thirty of them which have been revealed to be nearly identi-
cal to the originals they replaced.

Collection: Alaska State Museum (II-A-5398).

JULY

AUGUST

JULY 1995

S	M	T	W	T	F	S
						1
2	3	4	5	6	7	8
9	10	11	12	13	14	15
16	17	18	19	20	21	22
23	24	25	26	27	28	29
30	31					

AUGUST 1995

S	M	T	W	T	F	S
		1	2	3	4	5
6	7	8	9	10	11	12
13	14	15	16	17	18	19
20	21	22	23	24	25	26
27	28	29	30	31		

Monday

31

1959 A federal bill to provide water, drainage, sewerage, and waste disposal systems for native people is signed into law.

Tuesday

1

1923 Birthday of Joe S. Sando [Jemez Pueblo], author of the book *Pueblo Nations*.

Wednesday

2

1855 A treaty is signed at Sault Ste. Marie, Michigan, to compensate the Chippewa for the destruction of their homes caused by the construction of the Soo Locks. They have yet to be paid.

Thursday

3

First quarter of the *Hand Rises Moon* of the Havasupai.

Friday

4

1540 Francisco de Coronado, in a letter acknowledging New World native political freedom: "By what I can find out or observe . . . none of the towns have any [lords]."

Saturday

5

1957 At an intertribal powwow held at Sheridan, Wyoming, Dolores Jean Shorty [Navajo] chosen as Miss Indian American.

Sunday

6

1975 President Ford signs a bill which extends provisions of the Voting Rights Act to include "language minorities," including Native Americans.

AUGUST

AUGUST 1995

S	M	T	W	T	F	S
		1	2	3	4	5
6	7	8	9	10	11	12
13	14	15	16	17	18	19
20	21	22	23	24	25	26
27	28	29	30	31		

Monday

7

1789 Congress declares: "The utmost good faith shall always be observed towards the Indians . . . their property, rights and liberty shall never be invaded or disturbed."

Tuesday

8

1947 Over objections from the area's Tlingit Indians, the U.S. government agrees to a timber sale from the Tongass National Forest in Alaska.

Wednesday

9

1836 For an annuity of £1,250, the Saugeen Chippewa cede 1.5 million acres bordering Lake Huron in southern Ontario.

Thursday

10

Full *Dog Day Moon* of the Yuchi.

Friday

11

1978 Congress approves the American Indian Religious Freedom Act: "It shall be the policy of the U.S. to protect and preserve for American Indians their inherent right . . . and freedom to worship through ceremonial and traditional rites."

Saturday

12

1972 Colombian Bari Indian leader Maurico Cobaira Bobrichora killed in a clash with white settlers on the Venezuela border.

Sunday

13

1960 The remains of George V. Nash [Winnebago], World War I veteran, reburied in Pontiac, Michigan. He had been removed the day before from his grave in a Troy, Michigan, cemetery because it was restricted to "Caucasians."

Jesse Cooday (Tlingit), UNTITLED, 1992; photo silkscreen, acrylic, and graphite on canvas, 27 x 27" (68.6 x 68.6 cm.).

Cooday created this work to honor his family, the Woosh Keentaan clan, and also Jay Silverheels, who played the role of Tonto on the television show "The Lone Ranger." Representative of the acculturated imagery that forms the basis of much contemporary Native American art, this painting combines the image of a classic Northwest Coast transformation mask with a horse and rider reminiscent of Plains Indian ledger art. Though some American Indians are opposed to such mixing, the history of American Indian art is marked by a synthesis and adaptation of forms and materials.

Collection of the artist.

**George Catlin, GROUP OF NORTH AMERICAN INDIANS, FROM LIFE, 1845;
hand-colored lithograph, 18 x 13 3/4" (45.7 x 35 cm.).**

———————

This portrait of an Osage warrior, an Iroquois, and a Pawnee woman was made by
George Catlin–attorney, entrepreneur, and painter–who traveled west in the 1830s
in order to record the customs and appearances of native peoples. Now considered a
visionary, at the time Catlin felt native cultures were in danger of being swept away by
encroaching white settlement. Catlin's North American Indian portfolio, a collection
of twenty-five images of Plains Indian life, including this one, is considered the rarest
American color document.

Private collection.

AUGUST

AUGUST 1995

S	M	T	W	T	F	S
		1	2	3	4	5
6	7	8	9	10	11	12
13	14	15	16	17	18	19
20	21	22	23	24	25	26
27	28	29	30	31		

Monday
14

1843 The end of the Second Seminole War, six years after the capture of the Seminole leader Osceola.

Tuesday
15

1991 The Canadian Supreme Court rules that the Teme-Augama Anishnabe have no rights to a claim of 6,000 square miles in northern Ontario, opening the area to mineral exploration.

Wednesday
16

1929 Birthday of Maurice Kenny [Mohawk], author of several books of poetry including *Greyhounding This America* and *The Mama Poems*.

Thursday
17

Last quarter of the *Start to Fly Moon* of the Eastern Cree.

Friday
18

1972 News reports state that over 100 Xavante Indians have died recently of flu and measles after the tribe came into contact with non-Indians working on the Trans-Amazon Highway in Brazil.

Saturday
19

1974 Members of the Ojibway Warriors Society agree to end their month-long occupation of the Anicinabe Park in Kenora, Ontario, occupied in protest over the treatment of native people by the Canadian government.

Sunday
20

1851 Calanapo, Habinapo, and other tribes cede an area of northern California.

AUGUST

AUGUST 1995

S	M	T	W	T	F	S
		1	2	3	4	5
6	7	8	9	10	11	12
13	14	15	16	17	18	19
20	21	22	23	24	25	26
27	28	29	30	31		

Monday
21

1871 By the Manitoba Post Treaty (Treaty No. 2), the Chippewa cede an area of southcentral Manitoba, and a portion of southeast Saskatchewan.

Tuesday
22

1949 The Saginaw Chippewa of Michigan and the Stockbridge-Munsee of Wisconsin become the first tribes to be released from government wardship and authorized by the government to administer their own affairs.

Wednesday
23

1969 Representatives of 46 tribes call for the ouster of Interior Secretary Walter Hickel, accusing him of "high-handed [and] inconsiderate" actions that adversely affect native people living on reservations.

Thursday
24

1888 Death of Ouray, the great chief of the Uncompahgre Utes.

Friday
25

New *Beard of the Corn Moon* of the Laguna Pueblo.

Saturday
26

In August of 1992, the state bar of Michigan dedicates its 16th Legal Milestone, which recognizes a Michigan Supreme Court ruling that affirms that tribal law and custom are legally binding in the state.

Sunday
27

1949 Birthday of Beatrice Culleton Mosionier, Métis author of *In Search of April Raintree* and other works.

**Nampeyo (Hopi-Tewa), BOWL IN THE SIKYATKI REVIVAL STYLE, c. 1900–07;
terra-cotta, white slip, pigment, 2 1/2" H, 7 1/4" Diam. (6.4, 18.5 cm.).**

———

Nampeyo's elegant pottery was inspired by archeological discoveries of ancient Sikyatki
prototypes. Her work, like theirs, is characterized by abstract animal designs: bear
paws decorate this bowl. Nampeyo became internationally recognized as a symbol of
Hopi culture in the promotional materials of the Santa Fe Railroad and the Fred Harvey
Company, who used her image to lure tourists to the Southwest. The insatiable
demand for handmade Indian pottery at the turn of the century may have been a
reaction against increasing mass production.

Collection: Hood Museum of Art, Dartmouth College, Hanover, NH;
Bequest of Frank C. and Clara G. Churchill.

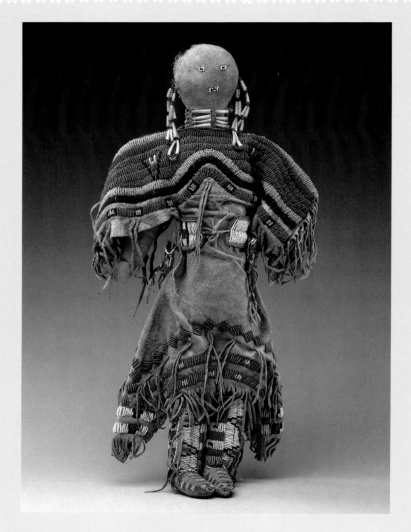

**DOLL (Sioux), c. 1890; cowhide, muslin, glass beads, dentalium shells,
19 7/8" H (50.5 cm.).**

Doting Plains relatives fashioned dolls cut from deerskin and minutely decorated with beads and quillwork. The dolls were true labors of love, and the effort and skill that went into creating them generally reflect the emphasis on appearance among the Plains nations. Typical of formal Sioux dress is the doll's jewelry and bead-embroidered yoke. The doll has only the merest suggestion of facial features, the rest of which were left to the imagination of the child.

Collection:Richard and Marion Pohrt. Photograph: Dirk Bakker.

AUGUST
SEPTEMBER

AUGUST 1995

S	M	T	W	T	F	S
		1	2	3	4	5
6	7	8	9	10	11	12
13	14	15	16	17	18	19
20	21	22	23	24	25	26
27	28	29	30	31		

SEPTEMBER 1995

S	M	T	W	T	F	S
					1	2
3	4	5	6	7	8	9
10	11	12	13	14	15	16
17	18	19	20	21	22	23
24	25	26	27	28	29	30

Monday
28

1676 The final remnants of King Philip's warriors surrender, ending King Philip's War.

Tuesday
29

1758 The State of New Jersey establishes the nation's first state reservation for Indians.

Wednesday
30

1945 Birthday of John Mohawk [Seneca], professor and author of *Exiled in the Land of the Free* and numerous other works.

Thursday
31

1946 The Indian Claims Commission is established to settle all outstanding native claims against the U.S. government.

Friday
1

1788 Frontiersmen from the self-proclaimed State of Franklin enjoined by Congress from trespassing on Cherokee land.

Saturday
2

First quarter of the *Manzanita Berry Moon* of the Yurok.

Sunday
3

1763 During Pontiac's siege of Detroit, a supply ship repels an Indian attack and resupplies the fort, saving it for the British.

SEPTEMBER

SEPTEMBER 1995

S	M	T	W	T	F	S
					1	2
3	4	5	6	7	8	9
10	11	12	13	14	15	16
17	18	19	20	21	22	23
24	25	26	27	28	29	30

Monday

4

Labor Day

1954 President Eisenhower signs a bill authorizing "termination" of federal supervision over several native groups in Utah.

Tuesday

5

1877 Death of Oglala Sioux warrior Crazy Horse from an army bayonet wound he received while "resisting arrest." With him died the dream of the Sioux to live free from government control.

Wednesday

6

1938 Birthday of Joan Peabody Tower, the first woman and the first Native American to win the prestigious Grawemeyer Award for original music composition.

Thursday

7

1850 Treaty with Canadian native people signed at Sault Ste. Marie, Ontario, ceding much territory along the northern shores of Lakes Huron and Superior.

Friday

8

Full *Little Chestnut Moon* of the Muskogee.

Saturday

9

1879 In the opening salvo of the Victorio War, the Mimbres Apache leader Victorio and about 60 warriors attack an Army cavalry unit near Ojo Caliente, in far western New Mexico.

Sunday

10

1836 Flat Mouth, Ojibwe chief, on Americans: "The Americans plan to treat us as they treat their black people. They do not come to see how we are. . . . I know why they do not come. It is because we are poor."

Mariá Sebastiana (Chumash), PRESENTATION BOWL, early nineteenth century;
juncus reed, 4 1/2"H, 15" Diam. (10.2, 38.1 cm.)

The Chumash of southern California created outstanding baskets that were avidly collected by the Spanish, who established five missions on Chumash land and pressed the basket
makers into their service. This rare basket is one of a group of only four inscribed baskets
bearing designs from Spanish colonial coins. It features four representations of an
eighteenth-century coin featuring the Royal Crown above double globes, the Old and
New World hemispheres. The inscription in translation reads "Mariá Sebastiana Indian
of the Mission of the Seraphic Doctor San Buenaventura, I made this."

Courtesy: Eleanor Tulman Hancock, Inc. Photograph: Allan Finkelman.

Edward Sheriff Curtis, GERONIMO, 1905; gravure, image: 16 x 12" (40.6 x 30.5 cm.).

After making his mark as a society photographer, Edward S. Curtis began to make images of and about American Indians in 1899. His opus, *The North American Indian* portfolio, consisted of approximately 2,500 images produced over a thirty-year period at a cost of one million dollars. After a period of obscurity, Curtis's work is currently at center stage. Some hold that Curtis's posed images are highly romanticized views that bear little relation to the lives he portrayed. Others treasure Curtis's photographs as proud portraits of deceased Indian ancestors unrecorded in any other medium. This photograph of famed Apache warrior Geronimo was taken on the day before he marched in President Theodore Roosevelt's inaugural parade.

Collection: Quintana Galleries, Portland, Oregon.

SEPTEMBER

SEPTEMBER 1995

S	M	T	W	T	F	S
					1	2
3	4	5	6	7	8	9
10	11	12	13	14	15	16
17	18	19	20	21	22	23
24	25	26	27	28	29	30

Monday

11

1980 A federal district court judge dismisses an $11 billion suit filed by the Oglala Sioux for damages to, and restoration of, the sacred Black Hills.

Tuesday

12

1924 Death of Charles Edenshaw, the most highly regarded carver of the Haida people.

Wednesday

13

1984 After nine years as a fugitive, AIM leader Dennis Banks turns himself in to South Dakota authorities to face sentencing on weapons charges.

Thursday

14

1816 After the War of 1812, a peace treaty is concluded with the Cherokee.

Friday

15

1906 Birthday of Mateo Aragon, lieutenant governor of the Santo Domingo Pueblo and vital spokesman for education among Pueblo people.

Saturday

16

Last quarter of the *Ducks Going Back Moon* of the Hare.

Sunday

17

1992 A memorial to the Navajo Code Talkers of World War II dedicated in Washington, D.C., commemorating the 50th anniversary of their establishment.

September

SEPTEMBER 1995

S	M	T	W	T	F	S
					1	2
3	4	5	6	7	8	9
10	11	12	13	14	15	16
17	18	19	20	21	22	23
24	25	26	27	28	29	30

Monday
18

1838 Under a forced removal order of Indiana Governor John Tipton, the Potawatomi are delivered to the "emigrant agency" on this date.

Tuesday
19

1986 Death of Harry J. W. Belvin, principal chief of the Choctaw Nation from 1949 to 1976, at age 85, in Durant, Oklahoma.

Wednesday
20

1977 Oren Lyons [Onondaga] to a United Nations conference on racism: "The equality of all life is what you must understand and the principle by which you must continue the future of this world."

Thursday
21

1832 As a result of the Black Hawk War, the Sauk Indians are forced to cede their lands in Iowa. This has come to be known as the "Black Hawk Purchase" and was concluded on this date.

Friday
22

1784 The Russians establish their first permanent settlement in Alaska on Kodiak Island. The settlement is harassed by the Inuit, but survives.

Saturday
23

Autumnal Equinox (First Day of Autumn)

1805 Lieutenant Zebulon Pike, acting on behalf of the U.S. Army, purchases land from the Sioux to establish Fort Snelling in Minnesota, marking the first of many treaties by which the Sioux lose their ancestral land.

Sunday
24

New *Corn in the Milk Moon* of the Acoma Pueblo.

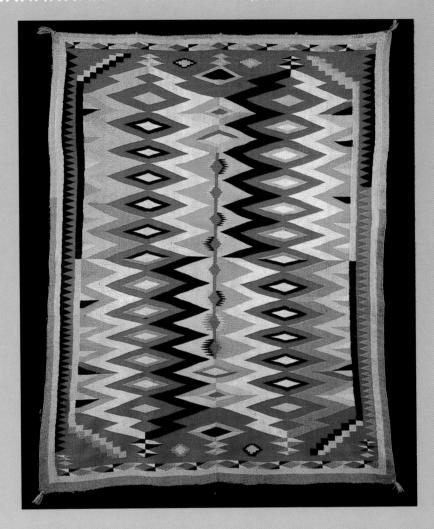

EYE DAZZLER (Navajo), c. 1880; Germantown yarn, 72 x 48" (182.9 x 121.9 cm.).

———

Navajos incarcerated at the Bosque Redondo reservation in New Mexico in the 1860s were given government-issue Mexican serapes that featured concentric diamond designs. By the 1880s, Navajo weavers had access to the brilliantly colored commercial yarns from Germantown, Pennsylvania, and combined the Mexican-inspired design with the vibrant yarns. This led to the creation of works of great visual power, all the more astonishing when one considers the despair of Navajo life at that time.

Courtesy Susan Parrish Antiques, New York City.

Larry Beck (Inupiaq), PUNK WALRUS SPIRIT, 1992; mixed media, 12 x 12 x 16" (30.5 x 30.5 x 40.6 cm.).

Instead of the wood, bone, and ivory used by his Inuit ancestors, Larry Beck makes his masks of materials readily available to him—chrome, aluminum, and plastic. This gleaming mask recalls the simplicity and visual power of the complex mask tradition of the Bering Sea Eskimos, whose masks not only entertained the community but also honored the spirits of sea animals.

Collection of the artist. Courtesy American Indian Contemporary Art, San Francisco. Photograph: Jay Daniel.

SEPTEMBER
OCTOBER

SEPTEMBER 1995

S	M	T	W	T	F	S
					1	2
3	4	5	6	7	8	9
10	11	12	13	14	15	16
17	18	19	20	21	22	23
24	25	26	27	28	29	30

OCTOBER 1995

S	M	T	W	T	F	S
1	2	3	4	5	6	7
8	9	10	11	12	13	14
15	16	17	18	19	20	21
22	23	24	25	26	27	28
29	30	31				

Monday
25

osh Hashanah

1913 Birthday of David Villasenor [Otomi], author of *Indian Designs* and *Tapestries in Sand*.

Tuesday
26

1990 The last of the Mohawk warriors involved in the months-long dispute at Oka, Quebec, surrender to government authorities.

Wednesday
27

1972 The first section of the controversial Trans-Amazon Highway, running through traditional native homelands in Brazil, is opened for traffic.

Thursday
28

1542 California explorer Rodriguez Cabrillo lands at what is now San Diego.

Friday
29

1974 About two hundred native people, part of the Native People's Caravan, take over a vacant government building in Ottawa to protest the Canadian government's treatment of native people.

Saturday
30

1905 Indian Commissioner Francis E. Leupp: "The Indian is a natural warrior, a natural logician, a natural artist. Let us not make the mistake . . . of washing out of them whatever is distinctly Indian."

Sunday
1

First quarter of the *Moon When Leaves Fade* of the Siciatl.

OCTOBER

OCTOBER 1995

S	M	T	W	T	F	S
1	2	3	4	5	6	7
8	9	10	11	12	13	14
15	16	17	18	19	20	21
22	23	24	25	26	27	28
29	30	31				

Monday

2

1947 Birthday of Ward Churchill [Creek-Cherokee], author of *Fantasies of the Master Race* and numerous other works.

Tuesday

3

1873 By the Northwest Angle Treaty (Treaty No. 3), the Chippewa and Saulteaux cede the southwest portion of northern Ontario.

Wednesday

4

Yom Kippur

1754 Death from pneumonia of the Oneida chief Half King, U.S. ally in the French and Indian War.

Thursday

5

1992 Death of Rosebud Yellow Robe Frantz, Indian activist and grandniece of Chief Sitting Bull.

Friday

6

1965 The BIA announces that $1. million in scholarships have been awarded to over 1,700 native students for the 1964-65 school year, an increase from the previous year of over 400 students.

Saturday

7

1966 Birthday of Sherman J. Alexie [Coeur d'Alene], author of the book of poetry *The Business of Fancy Dancing*.

Sunday

8

Full *Turkey Moon* of the Natchez.

MOCCASINS (possibly Red River Métis or Cree), c. 1875–1925; hide, quillwork, blue wool stroud, yarn, 10 1/8"L (25.7 cm.).

In their great variety of shapes and decoration, moccasins epitomize the individuality of the many tribes of North America, each of which had a slightly different method of cutting and decorating its shoes. This is an especially fine and unusual pair of northern quilled hide moccasins. The abstract geometric and floral appliqués on moccasins, created by embroidering tiny glass beads or the quills plucked from slow-moving porcupines, were meant to make one's feet as beautiful as the grasses, flowers, and pebbles over which they walked.

**Oscar Howe (Yanktonai Sioux), WOMAN SCALP DANCER, c. 1964;
casein on paper, 24 3/4 x 18" (62.9 x 45.7 cm.).**

Oscar Howe's mature paintings marked a significant turn in the course of Native
American painting. Though trained in traditional Indian subjects, notably at Dorothy
Dunn's Studio, Howe struggled to find an authentic and individualistic voice and was
criticized by experts and collectors alike for breaking away from the accepted style
and content of American Indian art. In his fluid abstractions, Howe sought to capture
the essence of the Dakota way of life.

OCTOBER

OCTOBER 1995

S	M	T	W	T	F	S
1	2	3	4	5	6	7
8	9	10	11	12	13	14
15	16	17	18	19	20	21
22	23	24	25	26	27	28
29	30	31				

Monday

9

Columbus Day Observed and Thanksgiving Day (Canada)

1868 Resolution of the Indian Peace Commission: "Resolved . . . that military force should be used to compel the removal . . . of all such Indians as may refuse to go. . . ."

Tuesday

10

1949 ARROW (American Restitution and Righting of Old Wrongs) formed in Washington, D.C., with Will Rogers, Jr., as its head.

Wednesday

11

1990 The Carrier-Sekani Tribal Council files a suit in Canada's federal court to block construction of a hydroelectric project in British Columbia that the Indians claim will destroy salmon stocks in rivers on their reserve.

Thursday

12

Columbus Day

1982 President Reagan signs a bill that settles the longstanding water rights concerns of the Papago people. The bill assures that the Papago will receive federal help to construct an irrigation system and nearly $40 million for tribal economic development.

Friday

13

1969 *Indians*, a play by Arthur Kopit which chronicles the mistreatment of native people at the end of the 19th century, opens in New York.

Saturday

14

1980 Death of Wilfred Pehrson, Penobscot tribal governor and leader in their fight for restoration of land in the nation's largest land claim action, a claim for over 12.5 million acres in Maine.

Sunday

15

1988 The Lubicon Cree of northern Alberta block access roads to oil fields operating on lands claimed by the Band.

OCTOBER

OCTOBER 1995

S	M	T	W	T	F	S
1	2	3	4	5	6	7
8	9	10	11	12	13	14
15	16	17	18	19	20	21
22	23	24	25	26	27	28
29	30	31				

Monday

16

Last quarter of the *Traveling Moon* of the Menominee.

Tuesday

17

1973 Pedro Bissonette, 33, veteran of the Wounded Knee Occupation, shot and killed by a BIA officer while "resisting arrest."

Wednesday

18

1865 Comanche and Kiowa cede central Texas.

Thursday

19

1841 Surrender of the Tallahassee chief Tigertail (Thlocko Tustenuggee) after his battle against forced removal west. He dies the next year in New Orleans during shipment to Indian Territory.

Friday

20

1832 The Chickasaw Nation, at the Treaty of Pontitock Creek, agrees to cede northern Mississippi and move west of the Mississippi River.

Saturday

21

Native Americans protest during the October 1991 World Series in Atlanta, citing the name of the Atlanta team and its fans' use of the "tomahawk chop" as demeaning to native people.

Sunday

22

1934 Birthday of Gerald Vizenor [Chippewa], author of *Bearheart: The Heirship Chronicles, Earthdivers*, and several other works of fiction and nonfiction.

Maria Martinez and Santana Martinez (San Ildefonso), BLACK-ON-BLACK FEATHER PLATE, c. 1950; earthenware, 12" Diam. (30.5 cm.).

At the turn of the century, Maria Martinez and her husband, Julian, were at the forefront of a new generation of potters who began making pots based on the shards of ancient ceramics unearthed by archeologists. This plate, made by Maria and her daughter-in-law Santana, is a graceful later example of the lustrous black-on-black ware resulting from Maria's innovative firing, a technique she shared with other members of her tribe. The new pottery was championed by the School of American Research, which in 1922 introduced the annual event now known as the Santa Fe Indian Market.

Courtesy Andrea Fisher Fine Pottery, Santa Fe. Photograph: Herb Lotz.

MAN'S SHIRT (Blackfeet), late nineteenth century; hide, quills, beads, hair, metal cones, human hair, pigment, cotton thread, 32 1/4"L, 61"W (82, 155 cm.).

During the reservation period, which began in the 1870s, the quality of ornamented objects remained high as the people clung to those items that reaffirmed their identity and spiritual values. A highly decorated shirt such as this one was a measure of prestige and worn on special occasions. Today, the love and labor required for such work is usually focused on the creation of the highly individualized costumes worn at powwows— celebrations used to visit with family and friends and again reaffirm one's Indian identity.

Collection: Glenbow Museum, Calgary (AF83).

OCTOBER

OCTOBER 1995

S	M	T	W	T	F	S
1	2	3	4	5	6	7
8	9	10	11	12	13	14
15	16	17	18	19	20	21
22	23	24	25	26	27	28
29	30	31				

Monday

23

New *Dust in the Face Moon* of the Cheyenne.

Tuesday

24

1969 Five thousand acres of Puget Sound beach and shoreline declared closed to non-natives by the Lummi Indians, who claim that the area is being abused.

Wednesday

25

1976 The Indian Brotherhood of the Northwest Territories files a claim to 450,000 square miles. The Brotherhood hopes to establish "a government roughly equal in status" to a province.

Thursday

26

1972 Caravans leave Seattle, Los Angeles, and San Francisco for Washington, D.C., on the Trail of Broken Treaties to draw attention to native issues and concerns.

Friday

27

1990 Congress passes the Indian Arts and Crafts Act of 1990, which is designed to protect the authenticity of Native American art.

Saturday

28

1932 U.S. Dept. of Interior removes Papago tribal lands from mineral exploration. This order was later rescinded by the Indian Reorganization Act of 1934.

Sunday

29

1832 The Wea agree to cede their lands and move west of the Mississippi River.

OCTOBER
NOVEMBER

OCTOBER 1995

S	M	T	W	T	F	S
1	2	3	4	5	6	7
8	9	10	11	12	13	14
15	16	17	18	19	20	21
22	23	24	25	26	27	28
29	30	31				

NOVEMBER 1995

S	M	T	W	T	F	S
			1	2	3	4
5	6	7	8	9	10	11
12	13	14	15	16	17	18
19	20	21	22	23	24	25
26	27	28	29	30		

Monday
30

First quarter of the *Frost on the Grass Moon* of the Kaniagmiut.

Tuesday
31

Halloween

1978 Canadian federal government and Inuit sign a pact which grants the Inuit control of 37,000 square miles of land in the western Arctic.

Wednesday
1

1984 The Canadian Supreme Court rules in favor of the Musqueam Indian Band who claimed that the federal government misled them in 1957 when it leased Musqueam land to golf course developers at very low rates.

Thursday
2

1903 Birthday of Elon "Chief" Hogsett [Cherokee], Detroit pitcher for eight years in the late 1920s and early 1930s.

Friday
3

1883 U.S. Supreme Court decides that an Indian is by birth an alien and a dependent of the U.S. government.

Saturday
4

1791 Two thousand Indians under Red Jacket [Mississayo] and Little Turtle [Miami] defeat the forces of General Arthur St. Clair near Fort Recovery, Ohio. Out of 1,400 soldiers, 632 are killed, 264 wounded.

Sunday
5

1981 Aboriginal rights provisions dropped from proposed Canadian Constitution. After intense public pressure the provisions are reinstated, by amendment, in June of 1984.

Nathan Youngblood (Santa Clara), SANTA CLARA RED AND SIENNA CARVED JAR, 1990; ceramic, 12"H, 9" Diam. (30.5, 22.9 cm.).

After traveling the world, Youngblood returned to his family's pueblo to study pottery with his grandmother, Margaret Tafoya, one of the doyennes of Southwest ceramics. In the 1920s, Tafoya innovated deep-relief carving on her pottery, now a signature style of the Santa Clara Pueblo. Youngblood expands upon this tradition, creating calligraphic surfaces that reveal the influences of many cultural traditions, especially that of Japanese carved jade sculpture.

Courtesy Gallery 10, Scottsdale and Santa Fe. Photograph: Roger M. Short.

HEADSTALL AND SADDLE BLANKET (Navajo), nineteenth century; headstall: sterling silver, original leather, full size.

Around 1870, Navajo men began to work in silver, a craft for which they became renowned. The first pieces made were simply hammered American silver dollars—acquired at trading posts—a practice that was ultimately forbidden by the government. Their repertoire quickly expanded to include engraving, casting, and stamping. Essential as well to the legend and life of the American Indian was the horse, which on festive occasions was bedecked with symbols depicting the wealth of its owner, which would have included spectacular silver trappings such as this headstall.

Courtesy: Eleanor Tulman Hancock, Inc. Photograph: Allan Finkelman.

NOVEMBER

NOVEMBER 1995

S	M	T	W	T	F	S
			1	2	3	4
5	6	7	8	9	10	11
12	13	14	15	16	17	18
19	20	21	22	23	24	25
26	27	28	29	30		

Monday

6

1858 Indian Commissioner Charles E. Mix on reservation policy: ". . . treaties [ceded] large tracts of country, which were needed . . . and [moved Indians to] more suitable locations, where they could be controlled and domesticated."

Tuesday

7

Election Day

Full *Great Hard Times Moon* of the Iroquois.

Wednesday

8

1938 Birthday of Johnny Yesno [Ojibway], radio producer, broadcaster, actor.

Thursday

9

1972 A federal court finds that the Interior Department has violated its trust responsibility and treaty obligations by allowing water to be diverted from Pyramid Lake, the central economic resource of the Paiute people.

Friday

10

1777 Chief Cornstalk and other Shawnee being held hostage in Fort Randolph, Virginia, murdered by soldiers in revenge for a Mingo attack on other soldiers away from the fort.

Saturday

11

Veterans Day and Remembrance Day (Canada)

1986 Commemorating the estimated 43,000 Native Americans who served in Vietnam, the Grandfather Plaque is dedicated in a ceremony at Arlington National Cemetery.

Sunday

12

1950 Birthday of Ray Young Bear [Mesquaki], poet and author of *Black Eagle Child*.

NOVEMBER

NOVEMBER 1995

S	M	T	W	T	F	S
			1	2	3	4
5	6	7	8	9	10	11
12	13	14	15	16	17	18
19	20	21	22	23	24	25
26	27	28	29	30		

Monday

13

1989 Bullet holes are discovered i
the windows of *The People's Voice*, a
Akwasasne newspaper, during dis
putes over gambling on their
reserve in upstate New York.

Tuesday

14

1942 Birthday of Annharte (Mari
Baker) [Saulteaux], author of the
poetry collection *Being on the Moon*.

Wednesday

15

Last quarter of the *Moon When the
White Salmon Run* of the Sanpoil.

Thursday

16

1990 President Bush signs a bill
designed to protect Native
American grave sites and orders
that remains and cultural artifacts
taken from grave sites are to be
returned to the tribes for reburial.

Friday

17

1785 Through strong drink, two
Creek subchiefs are induced to sign
a treaty ceding a large portion of
Creek land. The treaty was repudi-
ated by the Creek Nation.

Saturday

18

1981 Declaration of the First
Nations of Canada: "The creator
gave us our spiritual beliefs, our
languages, our culture, and a place
on Mother Earth which provided u
with all our needs [which] cannot
be altered by any other Nation."

Sunday

19

1981 Led by the Ojibway chief
Shingwauk, about 1,000 native peo
ple demonstrate in Ottawa to
protest the dropping of a native
rights clause from the proposed
Canadian Constitution.

FROG CREST HELMET, (Tlingit, Kisadi Clan), nineteenth century; wood, spruce root, pigment, abalone, ermine skin, 12"H (30.5 cm.).

This spectacular hat is co-owned by the Alaska State Museum and the Kisadi people who may borrow it for significant ceremonies, such as a potlatch, when such regalia is worn. The hat would be worn by an elder who would dance at the ceremony as well as deliver an oration. The frog is the crest of the Kisadi clan, although, curiously, no frogs are found in that part of the world.

Collection: Alaska State Museum (II-B-1840).

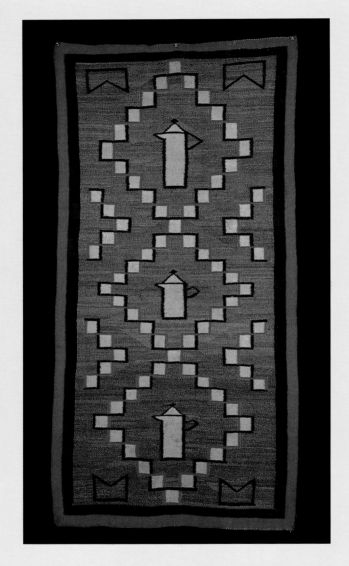

COFFEEPOTS RUG (Navajo), 1925–35; handspun wool, 72 x 36" (182.9 x 91.4 cm.).

Southwestern culture has always been influenced by, and has influenced, the dominant culture as described by postcards, magazines, and movies. Pictorial rugs, such as this charming example, were inspired by contact with white traders. This rug celebrates the coffeepot, a staple of the cowboy's campfire.

NOVEMBER

NOVEMBER 1995

S	M	T	W	T	F	S
			1	2	3	4
5	6	7	8	9	10	11
12	13	14	15	16	17	18
19	20	21	22	23	24	25
26	27	28	29	30		

Monday
20

1978 Two native people win seats on the Yukon Territorial Assembly, a first for that assembly.

Tuesday
21

A reorganization of the BIA designed to put the agency in touch with the people it serves is announced in November of 1970. The 11 area directors' positions are eliminated as part of the planned reorganization.

Wednesday
22

New *Bears Paw the Ground Moon* of the Haida.

Thursday
23
Thanksgiving Day

1868 Indian Commissioner N. G. Taylor: "Let us remember that . . . years of injustice, ... heaped upon them by our race with cold, calculating and relentless perseverance, have filled them with the passion of revenge, and made them desperate."

Friday
24

1972 U.S. Circuit Court rules that a BIA 99-year lease of Tesuque Pueblo land to a housing developer violated federal law.

Saturday
25

1992 In an attempt to settle a 100-year-old problem between the Hopi and the Navajo in Nevada, the U.S. Interior Department announces that it will cede over 500,000 acres of land in Arizona to the Hopi.

Sunday
26

1982 The Canadian government approves a split of the Northwest Territories into two political homelands, one for the Inuit in the east, and one for the Dene in the west.

NOVEMBER
DECEMBER

NOVEMBER 1995

S	M	T	W	T	F	S
			1	2	3	4
5	6	7	8	9	10	11
12	13	14	15	16	17	18
19	20	21	22	23	24	25
26	27	28	29	30		

DECEMBER 1995

S	M	T	W	T	F	S
					1	2
3	4	5	6	7	8	9
10	11	12	13	14	15	16
17	18	19	20	21	22	23
24	25	26	27	28	29	30
31						

Monday
27

In November of 1962, the California State Supreme Court rejects the religious freedom arguments of three Navajo and convicts them of violating narcotics laws by using peyote in their religious ceremonies.

Tuesday
28

1872 The government attempts to force the Modoc of northern California to remove to a reservation in Oregon. They refuse and the Modoc War begins the next day.

Wednesday
29

First quarter of the *Wind and Birds Screaming Moon* of the Makah.

Thursday
30

1992 Death of Donald Ames, descendant of Chief Buffalo, Army veteran, and chairman of the Bad River Band of Chippewa Indians.

Friday
1

1973 Date of enactment of legislation to restore tribal status to the Menominee who were "terminated" in 1961.

Saturday
2

1835 The Georgia Assembly on Cherokee removal: "From a knowledge of the Indian character, . . . it is confidently believed that the right of occupancy of the lands in their possession should be withdrawn."

Sunday
3

In December of 1985, nine Haida Indians are sentenced to five months in prison by a British Columbia Supreme Court justice for their role in a roadblock protest against logging on lands the Haida consider sacred.

**Allan Houser (Haozous) (Chiricahua Apache), SMOKE SIGNAL, 1993; bronze,
56 x 34 x 35" (142.2 x 86.4 x 88.9 cm.).**

Like the healing chants sung by his father, Houser's figurative sculptures project a
classic sense of unity, balance, and serenity. Critically acknowledged as the patriarch
of American Indian sculptors, Houser first studied with Dorothy Dunn in the 1930s at
the Studio in Santa Fe, the legendary painting school and spawning ground for
many Native American talents.

Collection: Glenn Green Galleries, Santa Fe and Scottsdale. Photograph: Lynn Lown.

Nora Naranjo-Morse (Santa Clara), A MISTAKE THAT TOOK ME SOUTH OF MY BORDER, 1992; clay, turquoise, silver, brass, 12"H (30.5 cm.).

Many ancient ritualistic objects incorporating precious metals have been excavated in New Mexico. Naranjo-Morse's figurine incorporates similar materials. Her work also raises questions about why American Indian art continues to be defined by such artifacts—long since removed from contemporary cultural and spiritual dialogue—and is relegated to ethnographic specimen cases in natural history museums.

Photograph courtesy American Indian Contemporary Art, San Francisco. Photograph: Jay Daniel.

DECEMBER

DECEMBER 1995

S	M	T	W	T	F	S
					1	2
3	4	5	6	7	8	9
10	11	12	13	14	15	16
17	18	19	20	21	22	23
24	25	26	27	28	29	30
31						

Monday
4

1991 By an Act of Congress, the year 1992 is proclaimed as the Year of the American Indian.

Tuesday
5

1818 Secretary of War John C. Calhoun: "[Indian] trade should [be] under the control of the Government, in order that [the Indians] may be protected against the fraud and the violence to which their ignorance and weakness would . . . expose them."

Wednesday
6

Full *Moon That Strikes the Earth Cold* of the Plains Cree.

Thursday
7

1792 The Mississauga cede a portion of southern Ontario bordering northern Lake Erie for £1,180.

Friday
8

1842 Birthday of Marie McLaughlin [Sioux], author of *Myths and Legends of the Sioux*.

Saturday
9

1992 Death of Dan Pine, Sr. (Shingwauk), respected elder of the Garden River Ojibway of northern Ontario. He was the last living great-grandson of Chief Shingwauk, War of 1812 warrior and signatory to the 1850 Robinson Treaty.

Sunday
10

1992 Mayan leader Rigoberta Menchú accepts the Nobel Peace Prize "as a recognition to those who have been, and still are in most parts of the world, the most exploited of the exploited ones, the most discriminated of the discriminated ones."

December

DECEMBER 1995

S	M	T	W	T	F	S
					1	2
3	4	5	6	7	8	9
10	11	12	13	14	15	16
17	18	19	20	21	22	23
24	25	26	27	28	29	30
31						

Monday
11

1989 The San Juan Paiutes gain federal tribal status.

Tuesday
12

1806 Birthday of Stand Watie, a Cherokee chief and Confederate general in the Civil War. He was the last Confederate general to surrender to the North.

Wednesday
13

1985 Ross Swimmer, former principal chief of the Cherokee Nation, sworn in as Assistant Secretary of the Interior for Indian Affairs.

Thursday
14

Last quarter of the *Brilliant Sun Moon* of the Chumash.

Friday
15

1970 U.S. government returns 48,000 acres of sacred lands, including Blue Lake, which was taken from them in 1906, to the Taos Pueblo Indians.

Saturday
16

1982 Canadian government and the Council for Yukon Indians reach an agreement on a longstanding land claim. The Yukon are to receive $183 million for the loss of 188,000 square miles of territory.

Sunday
17

1966 President Lyndon B. Johnson lights the National Christmas Tree, an eighty-foot spruce donated by the Fort Apache Indians of Arizona.

David Boxley (Tsimshian), LEGEND PANEL EAGLE, 1990; cedar, pigment, 30" Diam. (76.2 cm.).

———————

Highly decorative works like this contemporary wall panel continue the long tradition of wood carving and mask making in the Pacific Northwest Coast. Elaborate wooden masks were an essential part of the dance performances at the potlatch ceremony. Some masks allowed the wearers to transform themselves into various spirit-beings. The ability of humans to transform into animals and back again is central to the legend and spirituality of tribes of the Northwest Coast.

Collection: Quintana Galleries, Portland, Oregon.

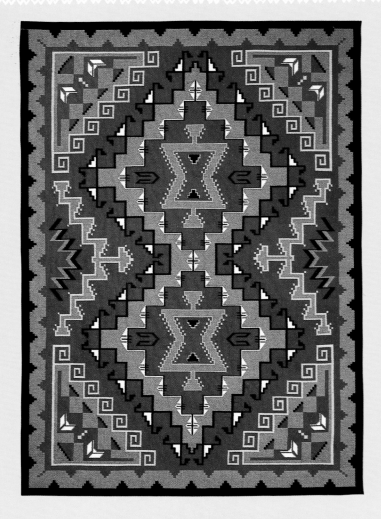

**Elsie Wilson (Navajo), GANADO WEAVING, 1984; wool,
83 x 57" (210.8 x 144.8 cm.).**

Once traders in the Southwest bartered staples for woven blankets with Indian
customers. Today Navajo weavings in diverse designs are just as avidly collected from
all parts of the reservation. The famed "Ganado red" is perhaps the best known of these
contemporary designs and features dynamic color combinations of red, white, black, and
gray. Elsie Wilson is from a family of award-winning weavers, who collaborate in
their designs as well as conduct a friendly rivalry with one another.

Courtesy: Christof's, Santa Fe. Photograph: Mark Nohl.

December

DECEMBER 1995

S	M	T	W	T	F	S
					1	2
3	4	5	6	7	8	9
10	11	12	13	14	15	16
17	18	19	20	21	22	23
24	25	26	27	28	29	30
31						

Monday
18
Hanukkah

1835 In the Battle of Black Point, the first engagement of the Second Seminole War fought near Micanopy, Florida, the Seminole rout a military wagon train.

Tuesday
19

1947 President Truman signs a bill authorizing aid of $2 million to the Navajo and Hopi facing unusually harsh winter conditions in the West.

Wednesday
20

1828 Georgia passes a law that states that after June 1, 1830, all laws of the Cherokee Nation are null and void in Georgia.

Thursday
21

New *Suffering Eyes Moon* of the Oglala.

Friday
22
Winter Solstice (First Day of Winter)

1830 The State of Georgia makes it unlawful for the Cherokee to meet in council, unless it is for the purpose of ceding lands.

Saturday
23

1890 Death of Ogista, son of Chief Shingwauk and himself an influential chief of the Ojibway people, at Garden River in northern Ontario.

Sunday
24

1931 Death of Flying Hawk, nephew of Sitting Bull and warrior at the Battle of the Little Bighorn. His memoirs were assembled in the book *Firewater and Forked Tongues: A Sioux Chief Interprets History*, published in 1947.

DECEMBER

DECEMBER 1995

S	M	T	W	T	F	S
					1	2
3	4	5	6	7	8	9
10	11	12	13	14	15	16
17	18	19	20	21	22	23
24	25	26	27	28	29	30
31						

Monday
25
Christmas Day

1611 Settlers under Sir Thomas Dale destroy an Apamatuks village on the lower Appomattox River in Virginia; the settlers erect the town of Bermuda Hundred on the site.

Tuesday
26
Boxing Day (Canada)

1959 Birthday of Elizabeth Woody [Wasco-Navajo], author of the poetic work *Hand into Stone*.

Wednesday
27

1872 Yavapai Indians massacred at Skeleton Cave in the Salt River Canyon in southern Arizona.

Thursday
28

First quarter of the *Going in Time Moon* of the Thompson.

Friday
29

1835 At the Treaty of New Echota, the Cherokee Nation cedes to U.S. all their lands east of the Mississippi, including northwest Georgia and parts of Tennessee and North Carolina, and agrees to move west of the Mississippi River.

Saturday
30

1906 Birthday of Louis Bruce [Mohawk-Dakota], Commissioner of Indian Affairs.

Sunday
31

1972 Navajo Nation announces a plan to incorporate a Navajo arts and crafts enterprise charged with organizing and marketing art and handicraft of the Navajo people.

**GHOST DANCE DRESS (Arapaho), c. 1885; tanned hide, eagle feathers, pigment,
57 1/2 x 35" (146 x 89 cm.).**

Herded nearly starving onto reservations, the Plains Indians were engaged in a nightmarish
struggle for their lives by the end of the nineteenth century. It is said that Paiute prophet
Wovoka, inspired by a dream, founded the Ghost Dance religion, which was practiced with
fervor throughout the Plains states. It was believed that performing the Ghost Dance would
restore the good life—of peace, family, and plentiful buffalo. Dancers wore special clothing
like this dress painted with symbols such as circles and stars. Regarded by the federal
government as a dangerous resistance movement, the Ghost Dance reached its tragic
culmination in the massacre at Wounded Knee.

Peter Jones (Beaver Clan, Onondaga), OLD SONGS, 1991; stoneware,
25 x 9 x 9" (63.5 x 22.9 x 22.9 cm.).

———

Born on the Cattaraugus Indian Reservation in western New York, Peter Jones returned
to the reservation, like many contemporary Native American artists who had left to obtain
an education, in order to capture in his art a way of life that is rapidly disappearing.
This evocative work depicts an elder holding an Iroquois horn rattle, sweet grass, and a
carved fetish. It celebrates their songs and mourns the passing of traditional ways of life.

Courtesy American Indian Contemporary Art, San Francisco. Photograph: Jay Daniel.

JANUARY

JANUARY 1996

S	M	T	W	T	F	S
	1	2	3	4	5	6
7	8	9	10	11	12	13
14	15	16	17	18	19	20
21	22	23	24	25	26	27
28	29	30	31			

Monday

1

ew Year's Day

1990 Death of Ben Reifel, the first Sioux elected to the U.S. House of Representatives. He also held a doctorate from Harvard University and was a lieutenant colonel in World War II.

Tuesday

2

1969 A warrant is issued for the arrest of native fisher Rick Hoy for "illegal fishing" in the treaty waters in Washington State.

Wednesday

3

In January of 1973, the U.S. government officially rejects the 20 demands made by the Trail of Broken Promises occupiers of the BIA building in November of 1972.

Thursday

4

1950 Birthday of Moses Jumper, Jr. [Seminole], poet and author of the book *Echoes in the Wind*.

Friday

5

Full *Little Bud Moon* of the Kiowa.

Saturday

6

1992 The Canadian government apologizes to the survivors of 17 Inuit families who were moved from Quebec to the Arctic and left there without adequate food or shelter in a government attempt to assert sovereignty over the Arctic area.

Sunday

7

1934 Birthday of Jack Forbes [Powhatan-Delaware], poet, essayist, and author of many books on Native America.

PORT GAMBLE
JAMESTOWN KLALLAM
LOWER ELWHA
MAKAH
OZETTE
QUILEUTE
HOH
QUINAULT
SQUAXIN ISLAND
SHOALWATER BAY
CHEHALIS

SWINOMISH
LUMMI
NOOKSACK
UPPER SKAGIT
STILLAGUAMISH
TULALIP
SAUK SUIATTLE
SUQUAMISH
SKOKOMISH
PUYALLUP
MUCKLESHOOT
NISQUALLY
YAKIMA

COLVILLE
KOOTENAI
KALISPEL
SPOKANE

BLACKFEET

ROCKY BOY'S
(CHIPPEWA/CREE)

FORT PECK
(ASSINIBOINE/SIOUX)

TURTLE
(PLAINS

SALISH/KOOTENAI
COEUR D'ALENE

FORT BELKNAP
(ASSINIBOINE/GROS VENTRE)

THREE AFFILI
(MANDAN ARIK

GRANDE RONDE
SILETZ

COOS LOWER
UMPQUA & SIUSLAW

WARM SPRINGS
TRIBES

UMATILLA

NEZ PERCE

NORTHERN CHEYENNE
CROW

STANDING ROCK
(SIOUX)

COQUILLE
KLAMATH
COW CREEK OF UMPQUA

BURNS PAIUTE

WIND RIVER
(SHOSHONE/ARAPAHOE)

CHEYENNE RIVER
(SIOUX)

YUROK
HOOPA VALLEY

KAROK

FORT BIDWELL

FORT HALL
(SHOSHONE/BANNOCK)

FORT MCDERMITT

PINE RIDGE
(OGLALA SIOUX)

LOW

NUMEROUS SMALL
RANCHERIAS

ROUND VALLEY

SUMMIT LAKE
WINNEMUCCA COLONY

DUCK VALLEY

NORTHWESTERN SHOSHONE

PYRAMID LAKE
RENO SPARKS

TE-MOAK

SKULL VALLEY

UINTAH AND OURAY
(UTE)

CARSON COLONY
DRESSLERVILLE
COLONY
WOODFORDS
INDIAN COMMUNITY

LOVELOCK PAIUTE
PAIUTE/SHOSHONE
YERINGTON
YOMBA
WALKER RIVER
WASHOE
BENTON PAIUTE

GOSHUTE

ELY COLONY
DUCKWATER

NUMEROUS SMALL
RANCHERIAS

FORT INDEPENDENCE

PAIUTE

UTE MOUNTAIN
NAVAJO

JICARILLA APACHE
SOUTHERN UTE

SAN ILDEFONSO
SANTA CLARA
PICURIS
SAN JUAN

OTOE/M

TULE RIVER

MOAPA PAIUTE
LAS VEGAS PAIUTE

PAIUTE
KAIBAB

SAN JUAN PAIUTE

HOPI

TAOS
POJOAQUE
NAMBE
TESUQUE
COCHITI

SAC

CHEYENN

SANTA YNEZ

FORT MOJAVE
CHEMEHUEVI

MORONGO
AGUA CALIENTE
MISSION INDIANS

JAMUL INDIAN VILLAGE

QUECHAN

COCOPAH

HAVASUPAI
HUALAPAI

YAVAPAI
COLORADO RIVER
FORT MCDOWELL
SALT RIVER

AK CHIN

YAVAPAI-APACHE
TONTO APACHE
ZUNI

GILA RIVER

JEMEZ
ZIA
SANTO DOMINGO
SAN FELIPE
SANTA ANA
SANDIA
CANONCITO
ISLETA
LAGUNA
ACOMA
ALAMO NAVAJO

MESCALERO APACHE

DELAW
APA
FORT SILL APA

TOHONO O'ODHAM
(PAPAGO)

SAN XAVIER
(PAPAGO)

PASCUA YAQUI

FORT APACHE

SAN CARLOS
(APACHE)

YSLETA DEL SUR

TEXAS KICKAPOO

ARCTIC SLOPE

N.A.N.A.

BERING STRAITS

DOYON

CALISTA

COOK
INLET

AHTNA

BRISTOL BAY

CHUGACH

KONIAC

TLINGIT

ANNETTE ISLAND
(TSIMSHIAN)

ALEUT